THE COMPLETE

ELECTRIC SKILLET—FRYPAN COOKBOOK

The Complete
Electric Skillet—Frypan Cookbook

by Roberta Ames

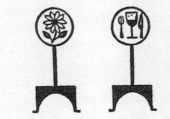

Hearthside Press Incorporated

Publishers • New York

TABLE OF CONTENTS

NEW TECHNIQUES WITH A NEW APPLIANCE, 12-20
  Using the Skillet, 13
  Cleaning the Skillet, 13
  Deep Frying, 14
  Shallow Frying, 15
  Braising and Pot Roasting, 15
  Sauteing, 15
  Poaching, 16
  Grilling, 16
  Pan Broiling, 16
  Stewing, 17
  Simmering Temperature, 17
  Chafing Dish Cookery, 17
  Keeping Foods Warm, 18
  About the Cover and Vent, 18
  Other Special Uses, 18
  Cooking Temperatures, 19
  Cooking Just for Two, 20
HOT HORS D'OEUVRES MADE EASY, 21-32
SOUPS, SAUCES AND GRAVIES, 33-52
SKILLET STYLE FISH AND SHELLFISH, 53-78
MEATS, PLAIN AND FANCY, 79-108
CHICKEN IN MANY VERSIONS, 109-132
VEGETABLES THE SKILLET WAY, 133-156
EGG AND CHEESE DISHES IN VARIETY, 157-164
THE PANCAKE AND SANDWICH BAR, 165-178
FRUITS, DESSERTS, SWEETS
  AND BEVERAGES, 179-190
INDEX, 191-196

Dedicated to

R. I. A.

THE COMPLETE
ELECTRIC SKILLET—FRYPAN COOKBOOK

NEW TECHNIQUES WITH
A NEW APPLIANCE

Cooking in an electric skillet or frypan (the words are synonymous here) is cooking at its best. Having tested thousands of recipes in my time—as cookbook editor for more years than I care to admit I probably am a champion recipe collector and tester—I can think of no appliance which fulfills so many different culinary functions either superbly or, as in the case of breadbaking for example, quite acceptably. (It would be ridiculous for you to bake in the skillet with an oven handy, but if one were not available—possibly at a weekend cabin—then the frypan would do very nicely). Recently I remarked to a friend that if I had to choose just one household appliance, it would be the electric skillet. She nominated the skillet as a close second to the washing machine. Agreed that it won't do laundry, the skillet will fry, braise, simmer, stew, pot-roast, pan broil, sauté and poach. It can pop corn, bake potatoes (softer textured than oven-baked ones), grill sandwiches, warm food, and act as chafing dish, toaster and sometimes as an oven.

I keep my frypan on a counter near the sink where it can be plugged in at a moment's notice. Since it is so easily washed, I find it practical for even a small job such as frying one egg. On the other hand, it has a greater capacity than most cooking vessels, so my company casseroles for ten or twelve are usually skillet-made. By the way, the skillet is then plugged in on the buffet table where it not only keeps the dish warm but also acts as the serving dish.

Using the Skillet

Plug the temperature control cord into the skillet, then into any AC wall outlet, 110- or 120-volt as directed by the manufacturer. Preheat the pan to the temperature noted in the recipe. The signal light will go off when the proper temperature is reached, but will continue to flash on and off through the cooking procedure as the proper heat is being maintained. When food is cooked set it at low or warm temperature if it will not be served immediately.

Cleaning the Skillet

Turn temperature off, unplug cord and remove it from the skillet. Wipe it clean. *Never immerse the temperature control in water.*

Let the skillet cool before you wash it, then wash both pan and lid with mild soap or detergent and hot water. It will clean quickly and easily. Fine steel wool makes stain removal easy and leaves the skillet gleaming.

A special finish keeps foods from sticking and no food has ever been burnt onto my skillet. If it should happen, however, scrape it off with a wooden spoon so you will not scratch the aluminum and soak in hot water until the food loosens. If necessary, bring water to boil in the skillet to make scorched food easier to remove.

Certain foods or alkaline scouring powders may leave a dark film on the surface. As far as can be determined by many laboratory studies, food is not in any way harmed by this film. However, to remove it, boil 2 teaspoons cream of tartar to every quart of water in the skillet for a few minutes. The boiling water should come as high as the dark film.

Deep Frying

Deep frying is cooking food by total immersion in fat. Only foods which are small enough to fit the skillet can be used for this method of cooking. Improperly fried foods are greasy, unpalatable, fattening because of excess absorption of oil, and tremendously irritating to the digestive tract. Since most of us, however, do enjoy deep-fried foods, there is every reason to learn how to prepare them the right way. Since the skillet controls temperature it is no trouble to learn how to fry foods properly. Here are some rules to observe:

1. Use a fat which does not decompose quickly ... vegetable oils and vegetable (not animal) shortenings are excellent. Butter, which has a better flavor than the oils, should be used only where frying is done quickly and not at high temperatures, since it decomposes readily.

2. The fat should be *hot* before the food is added, to avoid loss of juices and absorption of fat. Follow the temperatures given with the recipe.

3. Do not overload the pan with food to be fried ... fry one layer deep and wait for the light to go off between frying batches.

4. Because pan sizes and capacities vary, it would be difficult to give the exact amount of fat for deep-frying. For safety's sake, however, and to allow for foaming, do not fill the pan more than ⅓ full of oil.

5. When food is fried, lift it out with a slotted spoon and drain it on absorbent paper.

6. Fat may be used many times as long as it has good color and does not foam excessively. There is no transfer of flavor

from one food to another, so that the fish you may have fried last week will not affect the flavor of this week's corn fritters. Let the fat cool before handling it, then pour into container and refrigerate. Strain through filter paper or through several thicknesses of cheesecloth to remove any food particles. Add more oil as needed the next time you fry.

Shallow Frying

Food cooked by partial immersion in hot fat as compared with total immersion is shallow-fried. Southern Fried Chicken is an example. Follow the rules which apply under deep frying but use about ¼-inch layer of fat or even less.

Braising and Pot Roasting

Food is browned on all sides in a little hot fat which sears in the juices, then simmered with a little moisture added. Pot roasting refers to the cooking of meats, usually tough cuts of beef, by braising. A typical pot roast is given on page 87.

Sautéing

To cook at moderate heat by means of very little fat. The food particles which adhere to the bottom of the pan may be incorporated by swirling and scraping them with a liquid which then is served over the cooked food. However, where the recipe dish requires you to swirl and scrape the bits and pieces which cling to the bottom of the pan, I say so as a separate step.

Poaching

This describes the process of covering food with liquid which is then brought to the boiling point, without actually letting it boil. Eggs and fish are typical foods which lend themselves to poaching.

Grilling

If there were no other *raisin d'être* for the frypan but its use in making griddle cakes, I could honestly say it is worth having. What pure joy to breakfast with the rest of the family—not jumping up and down to watch and turn griddle cakes! And what melt-in-your-mouth, evenly browned pancakes result from temperature controlled baking.

I must make one point about pancake batter. It should have the consistency of light or coffee cream. When following a recipe for batter, keep this in mind and do not measure ingredients too accurately. In fact, there is so much variation in flour that it is pointless for you to do so. If you prefer thin delicate cakes as the French do them, use a thinner batter. For thick cakes (but of course you cannot fill them) use thicker batters.

Pan Broiling

Lamb chops and steaks which have a flat surface can be pan-broiled, that is, cooked in a very hot pan with little or no fat. Fatty fish like salmon are sometimes pan broiled but this is not a treatment about which I can be enthusiastic. It seems to me that even the fattest of fish needs some sort of sauce, even so simple a one as *à la meuniere* (see index for recipe).

Stewing

Foods to be stewed are cooked in a little liquid at low heat and for a prolonged period. They must simmer, not boil. Follow the procedure below to determine the simmering temperature in your skillet.

Simmering Temperature

Simmering means bringing food to the boiling point without letting it boil. The boiling point of water is affected by altitude, and there are other factors which make it difficult for me to tell you the temperature at which foods in your skillet will be *simmered* but not boiled. You can easily determine this for yourself, however. Pour in three cups of water, bring it to a full rolling boil and let it boil for a few minutes. Slowly turn the dial back until the signal light goes out. This should be the simmering temperature. (Liquid bubbles gently when light is on). Make a note of it here:

Simmering temperature for my skillet is:.........

Chafing Dish Cookery

A chafing dish is a double boiler made for table use. Any food for which a double boiler is normally recommended can be cooked right in the skillet. Sauces, for instance, require a temperature of 200° or slightly less. Cheeses and fondues, which are popular chafing dish recipes, can be made in an electric skillet. I like to use the lowest possible setting for melting cheese since it is a protein food which gets rubbery if cooked over too high a heat or for too long a period. The exact temperature will vary somewhat, but in general set the temperature at about 180° and raise it to 200° if necessary.

Keeping Foods Warm

Foods can be kept warm or reheated in the skillet, covered and set at 150° to 180°. To keep foods hot for longer periods, I wrap the cooked meal in heavy duty aluminum foil and seal the edges so that the package is airtight and no juice escapes. Then it can wait for hours if necessary, at 180°. If I have several cooked foods that have to be kept this way, I wrap them each individually in foil and keep them warm in the skillet.

Breads and rolls can be reheated right in the skillet. If they are somewhat stale, sprinkle them lightly with water, put cover on and heat at 225°. French bread can be buttered, sprinkled with garlic salt or cheese, wrapped in foil or put back in its original bag, folded over so it fits the skillet, and heated.

About the Cover and Vent

I hope you won't consider *not* buying the cover. You must have it for almost every method of cooking. Except where otherwise specified, keep the vent open when you cook for the escape of steam. (Even an oven provides for such an escape of steam.)

Other Special Uses

Have you ever seen recipes which call for a café brûlot bowl, or a corn popper, or waterless pan? Every single one of these pieces of equipment is expensive—yet the skillet can perform the functions for which they are bought. You really get triple value—or quadruple or more—when you buy your electric skillet. If you know a cooking accessory which is more versatile, please write in care of the publishers and let me know!

A Word About Cooking Temperatures

Have you ever had the experience, as I have had, that in cooking at the stove a sudden change in pressure occurs? Food set at simmering point is boiling away like mad, maybe through cumulative effect. Or food set with a low heat stops cooking—perhaps a gust of wind has extinguished the gas flame. When you cook in an electric-pan this cannot happen because a thermostatic unit controls the heat which is distributed evenly and quickly.

Therefore, with such accurate control it would seem that absolute cooking temperatures could be given for every single dish. Unfortunately this is not possible. Cooking is an art, and we cook the way painters paint—"as we see it."

As I see it, for example, eggs fried at 325° (which is usually recommended) get somewhat leathery. I prefer a temperature setting of 275°. Other factors complicate the selection of temperatures and times—if you reduce the amount of food in my recipe, less cooking time, and even a slightly lower temperature, will be required. Also, the same foods may vary from week to week in moisture content, maturity, etc., and these are important factors in cooking. If, in following my book, you are puzzled by the difference between the setting I recommend and the one recommended by the pan manufacturer, neither of us is necessarily wrong. You must cook as *you* see it—and not only see but taste, smell and even *feel* if you want to be a truly creative cook—as your skillet can help you to be.

Cooking Just For Two

Lucky you, to find among your wedding gifts an electric frypan! It probably will become your most useful appliance —the one which will help you prepare good food for every occasion and every meal.

Learn the basics of your new role as a homemaker-cook. Begin by reading the manufacturers directions which are enclosed with each frypan. The section on eggs will get you off to a good start. Read this chapter carefully too.

Entertaining Is Easier

Your frypan will be invaluable when you invite friends in. A cardinal rule when you entertain is this: plan parties that are easy to manage. Skip the fancy formal dinners which require a full staff to cook and serve. Concentrate instead on *fun* food . . . on things which can be cooked at the table to add spontaneity to the occasion. But do make certain you have everything ready and measured before you consider being the hostess-cook in public.

Whether you cook publicly or privately, however, this is certain: the frypan is perfected for almost every cooking need. It is an important—an indispensable—part of your culinary life.

HOT HORS D'OEUVRES
MADE EASY

18 RECIPES

Recipes in This Chapter

Buffet Meat Balls in Onion Sauce for 20, 23

Turkish Pepper with Yogurt Dressing, 23

Hot Cheese Hors D'Oeuvres, 24

Olive and Bacon Rolls, 24

Cocktail Turnovers, 25

Liver Knishes, 26

Chinese Egg Rolls, 27

Oysters in Bacon Blankets, 27

Bitochki, 28

Lobster Croquettes, 28

Cocktail Frankfurters and Pineapple, 29

Golden Crisp Butterfly Shrimp, 29

Fritto Misto, 30

Toasted Almonds, 30

Pop Corn, 31

Canapé Bases that Stay Flat, 31

Teriyakis, 31

Fried Dough Strips, 32

Buffet Meat Balls in Onion Sauce for 20

Shape 3 pounds of round steak into somewhat flat hamburgers about 1¼" in diameter, and sauté in butter in a skillet heated to 340°. Transfer to large platter. In skillet, cook 2 packages dehydrated onion soup according to package directions, but use half of the water recommended. When onions are soft, return the browned hamburgers to the skillet, and set on buffet. Serve with toothpicks, 1", hamburger buns (can be ordered from bakery), and bowls holding small slices of onion (use the centers only of medium or large onions and save the outside sections for deep fried onion rings), little pickles, hamburger relish, and ketchup. Let guests help themselves. Stays hot indefinitely in skillet set at warm or 150°. 20 servings. (If yours is one of the smaller skillets, keep half of the hamburgers and sauce in kitchen; transfer to buffet as soon as you can.)

Turkish Pepper with Yogurt Dressing

Remove the seeds from one pound of colorful green and red peppers. Cut them into strips or squares. Fry them in 3 tablespoons olive oil in skillet heated to 350°. Serve with a dip of lightly salted yogurt. Two garlic cloves, finely mashed, may be mixed into the yogurt.

Strips of eggplant, fried as directed on page 142, are also served in Turkey with a salted yogurt dip as an appetizer.

Hot Cheese Hors D'Oeuvres

½ cup soft bread crumbs
½ teaspoon salt
½ teaspoon pepper
½ teaspoon Worcestershire sauce
2 eggs, separated
2 cups grated Cheddar cheese
Fine bread crumbs
Fat for pan

1. Combine bread crumbs with salt, pepper, Worcestershire sauce, and egg yolks, then stir in cheese. Mix well.

2. Beat egg white stiff. Fold into cheese mixture. Shape into 1-inch balls. Roll in fine crumbs. Refrigerate until ready for use.

3. Heat pan and fat (filled to ⅓ the depth of the frypan, not higher) to 350°. Fry cheese balls until brown on all sides. Serve very hot—perhaps with wine as aperitif. Will make about 2 dozen. Cool the hot fat, then store to use again.

Olive and Bacon Rolls

Buy large pitted olives or remove the stuffing from the largest stuffed olives you can buy. (Dill pickle slices with centers taken out with apple core are good too.) Fill the centers with a sharp Cheddar cheese spread. Cut bacon slices in half and wrap each one around an olive. Fasten with a toothpick. Cook slowly in frypan set at 340° until bacon is done, turning as necessary. Drain on absorbent paper and serve hot. (These may also be served right from the frypan . . . partly cooked ahead, all the fat taken out of pan, then put back at 200° to finish cooking as needed).

Cocktail Turnovers

1. Use pie-crust mix following its directions, or prepare dough, page 183, for Southern Berry Pie. Roll out ⅛-inch thick, and cut into 2-inch rounds or squares. Or make two shapes, using a different filling in each. On half, spread 1 full teaspoon of any of the following fillings, moisten the edges with water, and pair off with remaining shapes. Press edges firmly together. Add fat to pan ⅓" deep. Cooking time: 3-5 minutes. Yield: about 25 turnovers.

2. Heat pan to 380°. When light blinks off, lower turnovers and fry until golden on both sides. Roll in paprika or parsley flakes. Serve hot with cocktails or soups. Allow ½ cup of filling for 25 turnovers.

Caviar Filling. Season caviar with lemon juice, grated onion and mashed hard-cooked egg.

Curried Lamb Filling. Combine minced cooked lamb with white sauce, season with curry powder.

Prepared Fillings. Liver pâte, or corned beef hash, are very good and very easy. Season well before using.

Chopped Tongue. Combine chopped cooked tongue with cream cheese, mustard, and grated onion to taste.

Chicken Filling. Combine 1 teaspoon sugar, 1 teaspoon cornstarch, 1 tablespoon soy sauce, ½ teaspoon salt, 1 tablespoon oil, dash of ginger, 2 tablespoons each of minced parsley and scallions. Spread over 1 cup minced chicken. Let mellow an hour before using as filling. Use as hors d'oeuvre for a Chinese dinner.

Cheese Turnovers. Grated cheese, a packaged cheese spread, or cream cheese blended with anchovies mashed to a paste are recommended fillings.

Liver Knishes

A knish is a little pastry filled with liver or mashed potatoes. This is an imitation, since it is made with bread, but it is delicious and easy.

> ½ pound chicken livers (fresh ones preferred—frozen livers have a grainy texture)
> 1 large onion, sliced thin
> 2 tablespoons oil or rendered chicken fat
> 2 hard-cooked eggs
> Salt and pepper
> 1 tablespoon brandy
> 1-pound loaf of thin sliced white bread
> 5 tablespoons oil for pan

1. Sauté onion and liver in oil or chicken fat in frypan set at 250°. Rest the livers on the onions so that they cook more slowly. When livers are barely done and still quite moist, turn off heat and let cool, then blend the eggs, livers, onions and fat from pan in an Osterizer, or put them all through the meat grinder using the fine blade. Season to taste with salt, pepper, and a tablespoon of brandy. Mix well.

2. Cut away crust from a loaf of thin sliced white bread. Roll each slice paper thin with a rolling pin. Cut into thirds.

3. Place a generous teaspoon of the liver mixture at the edge of each bread case and roll up. Wrap in wax paper and refrigerate until ready to use.

4. Heat oil in pan set at 350°, fry "knishes" about 5 minutes on each side. Serve hot. Will make about 60. Well seasoned, mashed potatoes may be used in place of liver, or in combination with it.

Chinese Egg Rolls

A very good recipe, these are crisp and nicely flavored.

½ cup cooked chicken, pork, or beef (or combination)
¼ cup cooked shrimps
2 large mushrooms
½ cup canned bean sprouts, drained
½ small onion
1 teaspoon salt
¼ teaspoon pepper
¼ teaspoon sugar
2 tablespoons soy sauce
1 teaspoon cornstarch
1 teaspoon parsley flakes
14 pancakes (see page 168 or 171)
4 tablespoons fat for pan

1. Put meat, shrimps, mushrooms, bean sprouts, and onion through the food chopper, using fine grind, or chop by hand (each food separately then blend). Add other ingredients (except pancakes and fat) and mix well. Place 1 heaping tablespoon in center of each pancake. Roll pancakes, folding in the ends as you roll. Refrigerate until ready to use.

2. Heat pan to 350°. Add fat and when it melts, brown rolls to a golden color, turning. Cut into thirds. Serve with English mustard. Cooking time: 5-8 minutes. Yield: 14 egg rolls.

Oysters in Bacon Blankets

Season oysters with salt and pepper. Wrap each one in a half slice of bacon, fasten with a toothpick, and fry in skillet set at 340°. Serve when bacon is browned. Allow 2-4 minutes.

Bitochki

    1 cup finely-diced cooked veal
    ½ cup finely-diced cooked green beans
    ½ cup butter
    Salt and pepper
    Flour
    Fat for pan ½" deep

1. With a fork, cream together veal, beans, and butter. Season with salt and pepper. Shape mixture into small balls. Roll in flour. Put fat into pan.

2. Heat pan to 350°. Lower bitochki into hot fat, brown on both sides. Remove with slotted spoon to absorbent paper. Serve on toothpicks. Cooking time: 2-3 minutes. Yield: about 30 balls.

Variation: Follow recipe above but use cooked chicken or turkey and mashed peas and carrots. Shellfish are also good: cooked shrimp, lobster, crab meat, etc. Season to taste, and be experiment-minded when you taste.

Lobster Croquettes

This recipe can be ad-libbed . . . that's the beauty of croquettes. Combine about 1 cup shredded cooked lobster or any leftover fish with enough cream of mushroom soup or a white sauce to moisten. Season with salt and pepper. Shape into rolls as thin as your middle finger and half as long. Roll in fine crumbs. Let dry. Fry in oil heated to 370°. Don't add the croquettes until the light goes off to indicate the fat is hot enough. Then brown croquettes for a few minutes and remove. Drain on paper towels.

Cocktail Frankfurters and Pineapple

This recipe can be made ahead and served hot without the usual last-minute flurry.

Sauté cocktail franks in skillet set at 300°, in a few tablespoons butter. If pan seems very greasy, pour off fat. Cut out small balls of pineapple with the small melon scoop and brown them in the middle of the skillet. Pierce pineapple with colored toothpicks. Keep everything on the buffet at warming temperature. Guests help themselves to pineapple pick, which they then stick into cocktail frank. The empty pineapple shell with leafy top put back on can be set in the middle of the skillet, surrounded by pineapple balls with toothpicks—franks making a border.

Golden Crisp Butterfly Shrimp

Golden-good, crisp treats

    1½ pounds shrimp
    1 egg
    ⅓ cup milk
    ½ cup flour
    ½ teaspoon salt
    ½ teaspoon monosodium glutamate
    Oil for pan ½" deep

Remove shells and veins from shrimp. Cut almost through each one, starting on outside curve. Flatten slightly to make butterfly shape, but be careful not to break shrimp in two. Beat together egg, milk, flour, salt and monosodium-glutamate. Dip shrimp in batter. Let excess drain off. Heat pan to 360°. Add oil. As soon as light goes off, drop in shrimps and let them brown on both sides. Allow a few minutes for each batch to be done.

Fritto Misto

Use the Tempura Batter given on page 73 but substitute 1 cup flour for the cornstarch. Among the many foods which are first dipped into batter then deep fried in the skillet (in oil heated to 370, about ⅓ of the way up the pan) are:

uncooked calves liver squares
canned artichoke hearts
large pieces of uncooked crab or lobster meat
thick slices of tomato
partially cooked flowerets of cauliflower and broccoli
¾" squares of Gruyere or Swiss cheese

In some sections of Italy, the foods for a Fritto Misto are also dipped into fine crumbs after the batter. Be sure in any case that foods are prepared in varying shapes and sizes for an interesting platter. Garnish with sprigs of parsley and radish flowers.

Toasted Almonds

4 tablespoons butter
1 cup shelled, blanched almonds, filberts or Brazil nuts

Heat pan to 300°. Melt butter. Add nuts, one layer deep, and fry until delicately brown on both sides. Remove with slotted spoon, and let drain on absorbent paper. Sprinkle with salt, garlic salt, ginger or curry powder. Wonderful with cocktails, fruit or vegetable salads, or slivered and sprinkled over cooked creamed asparagus, broccoli, cauliflower, green beans or spinach. Or toast nuts at the company table, spoon over ice cream which is just out of the freezer. It's fun for guests to watch even so small a cooking task as toasting nuts.

To Blanch Nuts: Cover shelled nuts with water. Bring to boil at 400°. Drain. Slip off skin by pressing nut between thumb and forefinger. Dry well between towels before frying. Cooking time: 1-3 minutes. Yield: 1 cup.

Pop Corn

Add 5 tablespoons olive or salad oil to pan, heat to 420°. When light goes off drop in corn kernels one layer deep (about 1 cup), cover and heat about 5 minutes until popping stops. Take out of skillet at once or pop corn will scorch. Drain on absorbent paper. Sprinkle with melted butter, salt, or garlic salt and serve. Repeat process, adding more oil if necessary, as often as the gang wants more.

Canapé Bases That Stay Flat

Cut bread into decorative shapes. Brush skillet lightly with butter and brown only one side of bread in skillet set at 300°. Spread filling over the untoasted side. (The bread base will curl if it is browned in oven or toaster.)

Teriyakis

  1 pound tender beef steak, cut into 20 bite-size pieces
  1 No. 2 can pineapple chunks, drained
  ½ cup pineapple sirup from can
  ¼ cup soy sauce
  1 clove garlic, mashed
  ½ teaspoon ground ginger
20 squares of green pepper
  3 tablespoons oil

The beef should be about ¾" square. Combine pineapple sirup, soy sauce, garlic and ginger, and spread over steak cubes. Set aside for an hour or so to let flavors blend. String up beef, green pepper and pineapple chunk on small skewers or toothpicks. Heat oil in skillet set at 300°. Brown skewers, turning as necessary; serve hot. 20 skewers.

Fried Dough Strips

> 1½ cups sifted flour
> 1 teaspoon salt
> 1 egg, beaten
> ⅓ cup water
> Corn oil, for frying

Sift together flour and salt, mix in beaten egg, add water; blend well. Knead mixture on floured board until smooth. Let stand ten minutes. Heat corn oil in electric skillet-frypan to 375° F., corn oil should be about ¾ inch deep but should not fill skillet-frypan more than ⅓ full. Roll out dough as thinly as possible. Cut in narrow strips. Drop dough strips into fat. Fry until bottom is golden brown; turn and fry on other side. Drain on absorbent paper. Makes about 3 dozen strips 1"x10".

SOUPS, SAUCES
AND GRAVIES

38 RECIPES

Recipes in This Chapter

Soups

Minestrone, 35
Chicken Soup, 36
Featherlight Matzo Dumplings, 37
Chicken Egg Drop Soup, 37
French Onion Soup, 38
Quick Celery Bisque, 38
Clam Chowder, 38
Shrimp Gumbo, 40
Bouillabaisse, 41

Sauces and Gravies

Medium White Sauce, 42
Thick White Sauce, 42
Cheese Sauce, 42
Cream Sauce, 43
Cucumber Sauce, 43
Curry Sauce, 43
Mock Hollandaise Sauce, 43
Hot Tartar Sauce, 43
Barbecue Sauce, 44

Basic Brown Sauce, 44
Mushroom Sauce, 45
Sauce Bigarde, 45
Beurre Noir, 45
Roux, 45
Giblet Stock and Gravy, 46
Champagne Raisin Sauce for
    Baked Ham, 50
A Favorite Spaghetti Sauce, 51
Sauce Florentine, 51
Velouté Sauce, 52

Dessert Sauces

Maraschino Cherry Sauce, 46
Chocolate Fudge Sauce, 47
Chocolate Sauce, 47
Coffee Sauce, 48
Lemon Sauce, 48
Orange Sauce, 48
Sherry Sauce, 49
Melba Sauce, 49
Maple Sundae Sauce, 49
Fruit Sauce, 50

Minestrone

For a simple supper set soup abubbling on the table. Serve with hot chunks of buttered French bread.

½ cup salt pork, or bacon, diced
1 clove garlic, mashed
1 small onion, diced
1 cup dried lima beans, soaked for several hours
1 cup fresh or canned tomatoes
1 cup shredded cabbage
1 cup diced potatoes
½ cup diced celery
½ cup diced carrots
½ cup chopped spinach
2 tablespoons minced parsley
8 bouillon cubes
½ cup spaghetti or macaroni
Salt and pepper
Grated Parmesan cheese

1. Heat pan to 300°. Put bacon or pork, garlic and onion in pan. Brown lightly. Add lima beans, tomatoes, cabbage, potatoes, celery, carrots, spinach, parsley and bouillon cubes dissolved in water. Now add 2 quarts of boiling water. Cover.

2. Reduce heat to simmering. Cover and close vents. Let *simmer* (not boil) 1½-2 hours. When vegetables are tender, add spaghetti or macaroni, salt and pepper, and let simmer for half an hour longer. Ladle into big bowls right from skillet. Sprinkle with grated cheese. Cooking time: About 2 hours. Six to 8 servings.

Chicken Soup

The electric pan is a perfect appliance for soup-making, not only because of its generous capacity, but also its large exposed surface makes scum easy to see and remove. Another advantage: heat can be controlled, the chicken can be simmered, not boiled, thus keeping it tender. (Boiling toughens meat).

> 1 4-5 pound fowl, cut up into 8 pieces (include heart, gizzard and neck)
> Chicken feet (ask the butcher for all he can spare)
> 3 quarts cold water
> 1 large carrot
> 1 cup celery leaves
> 1 leek or small onion
> 1 parsnip
> 2 teaspoons salt

1. Soak fowl in cold water to cover, then drain and sprinkle with coarse salt. Let stand for at least fifteen minutes. Rinse and wash thoroughly. This cleans the fowl and makes it unnecessary to throw away the first cooking water, which French chefs recommend. (Too much flavor goes into the drain with the discarded first water).

2. Clean the chicken feet by covering them with cold water in pan, and bringing water to boil. When water boils, turn off heat and remove feet one at a time. Dip each under cool water and peel off skin with a knife.

3. Put fowl and chicken feet in clean electric pan with cold water to cover, bring to boil at highest temperature setting. When water boils, spoon off the scum from the top, add vegetables, cover pan, close vents, and continue cooking at simmering point until chicken is tender, about 3 hours in all.

4. Discard all vegetables except carrot and, if possible, refrigerate soup (chicken in separate dish) so that fat will

solidify, making it easy to remove. Heat soup in covered pan at high heat, then reduce to simmering and add chicken to serve it warm. (Or save chicken and use for making salad or other dishes.)

5. Float a slice or two of cooked carrot in each soup plate. Cooked egg noodles or rice are usual accompaniments.

Featherlight Matzo Dumplings

Knaidlach—pronounce the k—are drained and served with chicken soup or as a substitute for a starchy vegetable.

Combine 3 eggs, 4 tablespoons rendered chicken fat, and 1 cup matzo meal. Beat well. Stir in a scant ½ cup water to make a stiff batter. Add 1 teaspoon salt and a dash of ginger (optional). Cover and refrigerate for several hours. Half an hour before serving, wet hands with cold water so batter does not stick to them and shape into balls. Fill frypan with as much water as it can comfortably hold, allowing for boiling, and bring it to quick boil at highest temperature. Salt it, add dumplings, reduce heat to 250° and cook for 30 minutes.

Chicken Egg Drop Soup

    4 cups seasoned chicken stock or soup
    4 eggs, beaten
    2 teaspoons soy sauce
    ½ teaspoon salt
    ¼ cup finely minced scallion (white and green)

Heat the chicken stock in covered skillet set at 300° then turn off heat. Give the eggs another beating, then pour them into soup in a little stream stirring all the time. Add soy sauce, stir and serve in bowls with chopped scallions for garnish.

For a thicker Egg Drop Soup mix 2 tablespoons cornstarch with 2 tablespoons water, stir into soup before adding eggs.

French Onion Soup

    3 tablespoons butter
    7 large onions, cut into ⅛" slices
    6 cups chicken or beef stock (or 6 bouillon cubes dis-
        solved in 6 cups hot water)
    1 teaspoon monosodium glutamate
    6 pieces of French bread, toasted
    Grated Parmesan cheese

Melt butter in frypan set at 300°, add onions which have
been separated into rings. Cook until onions are transparent,
then add chicken or beef stock (or bouillon cubes dissolved
in hot water). Cover pan and set at simmering point for 1
hour. Add monosodium glutamate. Taste for salt and pepper.
This can be prepared day before and reheated before serving. Serves 6. For buffet service: Set 6 casseroles in a circle
around the skillet. Ladle out soup. Place a slice of freshly
made toast in each casserole and sprinkle grated Parmesan
cheese over it. Serve extra cheese to be sprinkled over the
soup at the table. Serve with hot savory French bread, buttered, sprinkled with garlic salt and warmed in a paper bag
in a 375° oven.

Quick Celery Bisque

        1 can condensed cream of celery soup
        3 tablespoons sour cream
        1 can condensed undiluted beef broth
    1¼ cups water
        2 tablespoons chopped parsley

Combine cream of celery soup and sour cream in frypan at
250°. Stir until smooth. Add beef broth, water, and chopped
parsley. Heat and serve. Serves 4.

Clam Chowder

Don't leave the thyme out of this soup—it is as much a part of the chowder as the clams are. Serve in a deep bowl with pilot crackers of course.

- ¼ pound bacon or salt pork
- 2 onions, finely chopped
- 1 clove garlic, finely chopped
- Clam liquor
- Salt and pepper
- Dash of parsley
- 1 teaspoon thyme
- Dash of sage
- 3 stalks celery, freshly chopped
- 1 quart milk
- 3 large potatoes, peeled and cut into small cubes
- 1 quart clams, cut in halves
- 1 tablespoon butter
- 2 tablespoons cream

1. Cut up bacon or pork and put into cold pan. Set temperature at 320°.

2. Let brown, then pour off all but 2 tablespoons fat. Add onions and garlic and let them cook but not brown. Transfer to platter.

3. Add enough water to clam liquor to make 1 quart. Pour into pan. Mix in salt, pepper, parsley, thyme, sage and celery. Set temperature at highest point to bring to quick boil.

4. When clam stock has boiled, reduce heat to simmering point, add milk and potatoes, cover, close vent and let simmer until potatoes are done. Add clams, butter and cream and serve hot. (If soup is too thin, thicken with crackers.) Cooking time: About 1 hour. Yield: 4-6 servings.

Shrimp Gumbo

¼ cup butter
2 tablespoons flour
2 cloves garlic, minced
2 onions, sliced
½ green pepper, thinly sliced
2½ cups tomatoes, canned
1 No. 2 can okra, drained; or 1 package frozen whole okra
1 6-oz. can tomato paste
4 beef-bouillon cubes
1 tablespoon Worcestershire
½ teaspoon chili powder
Pinch thyme
1 bay leaf
1½ tablespoons salt
¼ teaspoon pepper
4 cups water
2 pounds cleaned, shelled raw shrimp
3 cups hot cooked rice
¼ cup snipped parsley

In skillet set at 250° melt butter, stir in flour, and cook until brown. Add garlic, onions, green pepper; cook slowly until tender. Add tomatoes and rest of ingredients except shrimp, rice, parsley. Simmer, uncovered, 45 min. Cool; refrigerate.

To serve: Heat tomato mixture over medium heat till just boiling; add shrimp; simmer, covered, about 5 minutes, or until shrimp are done. Combine rice with parsley. Serve gumbo in shallow plates over rice. 8 servings.

Bouillabaisse

This is a hearty soup of the meal-in-one-bowl type. Serve a generous portion as a main dish for luncheon, with a fruit-salad dessert.

½ cup olive oil
½ cup thinly sliced carrots
1 large onion, sliced
2 pounds mixed fish such as haddock, bass, flounder and whiting
2 teaspoons salt
¼ teaspoon black pepper
1 bay leaf
Pinch of saffron
1 cup canned or fresh chopped tomatoes
1 quart boiling water
1 dozen clams
1 cup cooked shrimp, crab or lobster meat
1 cup white wine
1 small strip lemon peel
1 tablespoon chopped parsley

Preheat pan to 300°. Add oil and when it is hot sauté carrots and onion for a few minutes until soft and golden, not brown. Add the fish, each variety cut differently (strips and squares of varying sizes), salt, pepper, bay leaf, saffron, tomatoes and boiling water. Lower heat to simmering point and cook about 15 minutes until fish is tender. Add clams, shrimp, wine and lemon peel. Cook 5 minutes longer. Stir in parsley. Serve very hot. Float melba toast spread with butter which has been mashed with garlic over bouillabaisse. Be sure there is a variety of fish shapes in each portion. Serves 5 or 6. Cooking time: About ½ hour.

Medium White Sauce

Most recipes direct you to use a double boiler for making sauces. However this is not necessary if you maintain even low heat as, of course, your electric skillet can do.

> 4 tablespoons butter
> 4 tablespoons flour
> ¾ teaspoon salt
> Dash of pepper
> 2 cups milk

Heat pan to 200°. Melt butter, stir in flour, salt and pepper, taking a few minutes. Smooth out lumps with wooden spoon. Keep all of this activity in the center of the pan as much as possible. Slowly pour in milk at sides of pan, a few tablespoons at a time. As milk heats, keep stirring it into the center of the pan to combine with flour and butter. Continue stirring until sauce is smooth and thick, about 15 minutes. Use as a base for creamed and scalloped dishes, and for other sauces below. Keeps well in refrigerator. To reheat, warm milk and stir in sauce; let cook to desired consistency. One cup of sauce will cream one cup of cooked meat, fish or vegetables.

Thick White Sauce

For croquettes and soufflés. Double butter, flour, salt and pepper amounts but do not increase milk. Cook as above.

Cheese Sauce

When white sauce is done, add 1 cup grated American cheese, 1 tablespoon Worcestershire sauce. Simmer at 150°, stirring until cheese melts. When company drops in, dress up plain boiled spaghetti by making cheese sauce at the table so they can watch.

Cream Sauce

Delicious with hot cooked vegetables. To Medium White Sauce add 2 egg yolks, one at a time, then slowly stir in ¾ cup heavy cream and a dash of lemon juice. Heat and serve.

Cucumber Sauce

Excellent with poached salmon or any other fish. To cooling white sauce, add ½ cup mayonnaise, 1 tablespoon vinegar, and a large cucumber which has been peeled, seeded and finely diced. Stir in a drop of green vegetable coloring to make sauce pale green.

Curry Sauce

Follow recipe for Medium White Sauce. Add 1 teaspoon grated onion juice, 2 or more teaspoons of curry powder, and a thread or two of saffron which has been softened in a tablespoon of hot water. (The saffron adds color.)

Mock Hollandaise Sauce

Make Medium White Sauce. Turn off heat. Stir in 2 slightly-beaten egg yolks, 2 tablespoons onion juice, and slowly add 2 tablespoons melted butter. Sprinkle with paprika before serving. For any cooked vegetable. Delicious over open sandwiches of sliced chicken or turkey.

Hot Tartar Sauce

Serve on shredded cabbage, sliced cucumbers, or with fried seafood of course. To 2 cups of Medium White Sauce, when it is thick, add ½ cup mayonnaise, and 2 tablespoons each of minced sweet pickles, stuffed olives, minced parsley, vinegar and a dash or two of grated onion.

Barbecue Sauce

Pour the following ingredients into the frypan and bring to a boil at highest temperature setting: 1 cup ketchup, ¼ cup vinegar, ¼ cup Worcestershire sauce, 2 cups water, 1 teaspoon salt, 1 teaspoon celery seed, 1 teaspoon grated onion, 2 tablespoons brown sugar, dash of chili powder. Use to baste meat or chicken.

Basic Brown Sauce

    3 tablespoons oil or other fat
    2 tablespoons minced ham
    2 tablespoons chopped celery
    3 tablespoons diced carrots
    3 tablespoons chopped onion
    3 tablespoons chopped green pepper
    Few sprigs parsley
    1 clove garlic
    4 tablespoons flour
1½ cups meat stock or canned beef gravy
    ½ cup chopped tomatoes
    Salt and pepper

Heat oil or other fat at 200° and fry the ham and all the vegetables until they are well browned. Stir in the flour and be sure it is well dissolved. Gradually add the stock, a little at a time, and then the chopped tomatoes. Add salt and pepper, and then continue to cook until the sauce is "ripe" and thick. Strain through a fine strainer and use as the basis for many other sauces. (In the *cuisine classique*, this sauce is known as Espagnole Sauce. It is used in making many fine sauces.)

Mushroom Sauce

Sauté cup sliced mushrooms in hot fat in skillet set at 250°. Stir in 2 cups brown sauce and let cook together for a few minutes before serving. Serve with meat or chicken.

Sauce Bigarde

Excellent with roast duck. Very slowly stir in ¾ cup of orange juice to a cup of brown sauce, bring to a boil, then add 3 tablespoons orange rind (remove all the white first) cut into very fine shreds.

Beurre Noir

(Black butter sauce). Melt ½ cup butter (1 stick) in skillet set at 300°. When it is lightly brown, stir in 1 tablespoon tarragon vinegar and a dash of grated pepper. Serve over poached eggs. It is surprising how a little extra attraction like this, if made at the table and served sizzling hot, possibly with a grating of Parmesan cheese, over cooked cauliflower, will add distinction to your cooking. Yield: ½ cup.

Roux

Melt several tablespoons butter in frypan set at 200°, gradually stir in an equal amount of flour; cook for 3 minutes for a white roux. For a blond or pale roux, cook only until the color begins to change. For a brown roux, cook until the roux is light brown. Store in refrigerator and use as needed. Make a sauce by stirring into hot liquid left from cooking vegetables, and in other sauces and soups.

Giblet Stock and Gravy

So many women cannot be bothered with giblets, which is a pity because giblet stock is a delicious base for sauces and gravies and also for cooking rice. Apart from the flavor they add, giblets and organs are considered protective foods, and perhaps are responsible for the magnificent physique of carnivorous animals. I usually freeze the giblets as I buy chickens, then cook several pairs at once.

To make giblet stock, put several sets of giblets and necks, a medium onion, and the tops of celery stalks, in plenty of cold water. Cover and bring to a quick boil. Spoon off scum from the top, turn heat to simmer point and cook for about two hours. With a slotted spoon, remove and discard onion and celery. Put giblets and neck meat (not bones) through meat grinder, return to skillet and use in place of water to cook rice, or for creamed chicken dishes.

To make giblet gravy for roast chicken or turkey, cook the giblet stock quickly, uncovered, at highest heat in your skillet, reducing the stock to about 2 cups. Take 3 tablespoons fat from roasting pan and combine with 3 tablespoons flour. Stir into giblet stock and let cook until thickened. Serve hot.

Maraschino Cherry Sauce

    4 tablespoons cornstarch
    ⅓ cup sugar
    3 tablespoons water
    ½ cup cherry sirup (from bottle)
    Dash of salt
    1 tablespoon butter
    ⅓ cup chopped Maraschino cherries

Combine cornstarch, sugar, water, sirup and salt in pan. Heat pan to 300°. Let boil until thickened. Add butter and cherries. Serve hot over puddings. Cooking time: 15 minutes. Yield: 2 cups.

Chocolate Fudge Sauce

>   2 ounces (2 squares) bitter chocolate
>   2 tablespoons butter
>   2 cups milk
>   Dash of salt
>   ¾ cup sugar
>   2 tablespoons corn sirup
>   1 teaspoon vanilla

Heat pan to 200°. Add chocolate and butter. Stir until completely melted, then gradually add milk, salt, sugar, corn sirup and vanilla. Let cook 10 minutes. (A little sirup dropped into cold water should form a very soft ball.) Store in refrigerator. Reheat over low heat with a few tablespoons hot water. Serve with ice cream and cakes. Cooking time: 12-15 minutes. Yield: 3 cups.

Chocolate Sauce

>   1 pound grated chocolate
>   2⅔ cups water
>   2 tablespoons sugar
>   Few drops vanilla
>   6 tablespoons cream
>   2 tablespoons butter

1. Add chocolate and water to pan. Heat pan to 200°.

2. When chocolate melts, add sugar and vanilla and simmer for 25 minutes.

3. Turn off heat. Stir in cream and butter. Serve hot or cold. This may be stored in refrigerator for several days, and reheated when ready to serve. Good over plain cake and ice cream. Cooking time: 35 minutes. Yield: About 3 cups.

Coffee Sauce

1 cup strong black coffee
½ cup sugar
4 eggs, slightly beaten
1 cup heavy cream, stiffly beaten

1. Combine coffee and sugar in pan. Heat pan to 200°. When light goes off, add a few tablespoons of hot liquid to egg, then spoon back into pan.

2. Reduce heat to 150°. Stir sauce constantly. When mixture coats spoon, sauce is done. Turn off heat and chill. Before serving, fold in cream. Serve cold. Cooking time: About 20 minutes. Yield: 2½ cups sauce.

Lemon Sauce

2 cups water
2 tablespoons cornstarch
1 cup sugar
Dash of salt
2 tablespoons butter
1 teaspoon grated lemon rind
4 tablespoons lemon juice

Pour water into pan. Heat to 400°. Combine cornstarch, sugar and salt. As soon as water boils, stir a tablespoon or two into cornstarch then return mixture to pan. Reduce heat to simmering. Boil for 5 minutes, stirring constantly. Turn off heat. Add butter, lemon rind and juice. Nice with bread pudding. Cooking time: About 7 minutes. Yield: 2½ cups sauce.

Orange Sauce

Substitute ½ teaspoon grated orange rind and 2 tablespoons orange juice for lemon rind and lemon juice.

Sherry Sauce

2 cups water
4 tablespoons flour
1 cup sugar
Dash of salt
4 tablespoons butter
½ cup sherry wine

Pour 2 cups water into pan. Heat to 350°. Combine flour, sugar, and salt in a bowl. Slowly stir in boiling water, mixing until smooth. Put back into pan. Reduce heat to 200°. Continue cooking for 5 minutes. Turn off heat. Add butter and wine. Cooking time: About 14 minutes. Yield: 3 cups.

Melba Sauce

1 cup mashed frozen raspberries
¼ cup currant jelly
½ cup sugar
1 tablespoon cornstarch mixed in 2 tablespoons
cold water

Heat raspberries, currant jelly, and sugar until they are almost ready to boil. Stir in cornstarch. Simmer, stirring, until thickened. Serve with pancakes, and over vanilla ice cream and peaches in Peach Melba.

Maple Sundae Sauce

The children like this over ice cream—so do their parents.

1½ cups maple syrup
¾ cup undiluted evaporated milk
1 cup chopped almonds or pecans

Combine syrup and evaporated milk in a frypan set at 280°. When a few drops in cold water form a very soft ball, turn off heat and stir in almonds or pecans.

Fruit Sauce

Delicious poured over melon balls and grapes. Let fruit stand in sauce for an hour before using.

½ cup sugar
2 tablespoons cornstarch
½ cup pineapple juice
¼ cup grape juice
2 tablespoons lemon juice
3 tablespoons orange juice
Dash of cinnamon
3 tablespoons brandy or wine

Combine all ingredients except brandy or wine in frypan set at simmering temperature and let cook until thickened. Add brandy. Appropriate for most fruit cups.

Champagne Raisin Sauce for Baked Ham

Perhaps you had better read this recipe sitting down. It is not a dish for poor people but it makes a big impression even on the beatniks because man that sauce is like good!

1 cup raisins
1 cup white wine (sherry or chablis)
1 cup champagne (or 2 cups champagne and no other wine)
1 cup sugar
½ teaspoon salt
¼ teaspoon clove
¼ teaspoon cinnamon
1 tablespoon cornstarch dissolved in a little of the wine
4 tablespoons butter

Cover raisins with the still wine and let simmer in frypan for 5 minutes. Add all other ingredients and cook, stirring, until the mixture thickens slightly. It should not be too heavy or thick. Makes 3 cups and will serve 10 to 12. This is a good holiday sauce to make at the buffet table.

A Favorite Spaghetti Sauce

¼ cup olive oil
2 onions, chopped
½ pound chopped beef
1 clove garlic, chopped as fine as possible
3 tablespoons parsley (stems removed)
¼ cup dry white wine
Salt and pepper
2 teaspoons oregano
4 cups canned Italian tomatoes
1 4-oz. can tomato paste
½ cup water
1 pound spaghetti, cooked
½ cup grated Parmesan or Romano cheese

Sauté onions, chopped meat and garlic in oil in skillet set at 300° F. Pour in the wine and let cook slowly at 250° for ten minutes. Add the salt, pepper, parsley, oregano, tomatoes (if you use fresh tomatoes, peel them first then cut into chunks), tomato paste, and water. Cover, close vents and continue cooking for an hour and a half stirring occasionally. Serve very hot over cooked spaghetti which has been well drained. Sprinkle with cheese. Serves 6. If the sauce shows signs of drying out (it may during the last half hour) add water or chicken stock as necessary.

Sauce Florentine

Good with boiled noodles, plain poached fish fillets, and over hard-cooked eggs.

Make a Medium White Sauce (page 42). When sauce has thickened, add ¾ cup cooked chopped spinach, 2 tablespoons lemon juice and a dash of nutmeg.

Velouté Sauce

Use temperature setting of 200°. Heat 1 cup chicken stock, stir in 3 tablespoons blonde Roux (page 45). Cook about 3 minutes longer. Serve with chicken croquettes, baked chicken etc. A fish Velouté may be made using a fish stock rather than chicken stock.

SKILLET STYLE FISH AND SHELLFISH

39 RECIPES

Recipes in This Chapter

How to Shallow-Fry Fish, 55
How to Deep-Fry Fish, 55
Crisp Codfish Cakes, 56
Fish Loaf, 56
Fish and Chips, 57
Fish Sticks, 57
Flounder au Vin, 58
Fish à la Meuniere, 59
Court Bouillon, 59
Fillet of Flounder with
    Lobster Sauce, 60
Fish Steaks with White Grapes, 61
Tuna Casserole, 61
Halibut and Oyster Ragout, 62
Haddock and Mushrooms
    en Brochette, 63
Fish Dinner, 63
Clam Newburg, 64
Maryland Crab Cakes, 65
Fried Soft-Shell Crabs, 65
Crab Stew, 65
Jubilee Clam Fritters, 66

Crab Meat au Sherry, 66
Oyster Fry, 67
Oyster Terrapin, 68
Oysters in Blankets, 68
Sautéed Scallops, 69
Quick Tartar Sauce, 69
Shrimp Fra Diavolo in
    Rice Ring, 70
Shrimp Diavolo Flambé, 70
Steamed Shrimp, 71
Scampi Marinara, 71
Shrimps with Green Peas
    and Rice, 72
French Fried Shrimp, 72
Tempura, 73
Shrimp Jambalaya, 74
Lobster Newburg, 74
Lobster Cantonese, 75
Lobster Margarita, 76
Shrimp and Lobster Patties, 77
Scalloped Salmon, 78

How to Shallow-Fry Fish

Small Whole Fish. (Smelts, trout, etc.) Wash, dry with paper towels, leave on head and tail. Use any coating listed below. Heat pan to 370°. Melt ½ cup fat, brown fish on both sides, turning once. Allow 5-8 minutes.

Large Fish. (Bass, cod, etc.) Cut fish into steaks about 1-inch thick. Use any coating listed below. Heat pan to 360°. Melt ½ cup fat. Brown fish on both sides, turning once with pancake turner. Lower temperature to 200° and cook until fish flakes easily.

How to Deep-Fry Fish

Small fish and shellfish are delicious when deep-fried at controlled temperatures in your automatic skillet. Gash thick slices lengthwise and crosswise to speed frying. Use any coating listed below. Add enough shortening to pan so that fish will be half covered when immersed, but do not fill pan more than one third full of cooking oil. Heat pan and shortening to 380°. As soon as light winks off, lower fish, and brown on both sides. Remove with slotted spoon to paper to dry. Add just a few pieces at a time so fat does not cool. Do not overcook, since fish continues to fry in its own crust even after it is removed from oil. Deep frying time will be 2-6 minutes for most fish.

Flour Coating: (Easiest.) Dip clean fish in salted milk, drain, roll in seasoned flour, and fry.

Breading: (Crisp, brown crust.) Dip clean fish in seasoned flour, then into beaten egg mixed with 2 tablespoons water; roll in bread or cracker crumbs. Dry and fry.

Batter: (For fish with irregular surfaces.) Sift together 1 cup flour, 1 teaspoon baking powder, ½ teaspoon salt. Add 1 tablespoon olive oil, 1 egg, ½ cup milk. Mix to make smooth batter, dip fish in this, let excess drip off, drop fish in hot fat.

Crisp Codfish Cakes

1 pound (2 cups) codfish, flaked
2 cups (about 3 medium) diced raw potatoes
1 small onion
Salt and pepper
1 teaspoon minced parsley
1 egg, well beaten
Cooking oil for pan ¾" deep

1. Cook fresh or frozen (defrosted) fish with potatoes and onion in boiling salted water to cover for about 20 minutes until potatoes are tender. Discard onion. Drain thoroughly. Mash fish and potatoes together until smooth and well blended. Add salt, pepper, parsley and egg and mash some more. Shape into 8 patties, refrigerate if you have time.

2. Heat pan to 375°. Add oil. As soon as hot fry fish cakes in pan until crisp on both sides. Place cakes on absorbent paper to drain. Cooking time: 7-12 minutes. Yield: 4 servings.

Note: Serve with Mushroom Sauce, page 45, or canned tomato sauce.

Fish Loaf

Heat 1 cup milk. Add 3 cups mashed cooked or canned fish, 1 tablespoon butter, ½ cup soft bread crumbs, ½ teaspoon salt, dash of pepper and Worcestershire sauce, and 2 beaten eggs. Shape into loaf to fit pan. Brown in preheated frypan which has been lightly greased with oil (apply it with crumpled paper towel). Brown loaf on all sides, pour in 6 tablespoons water, cover and let simmer with vent closed for 40 minutes. Serve with Fish Velouté Sauce (page 52), or with the following Lemon Sauce: 1 egg beaten with 1 tablespoon sugar; add juice of 1 lemon and juices left in frypan from loaf.

Fish and Chips

> 3 baking potatoes, cut paper-thin and partly fried (recipe on page 100)
> Fat for pan ½" deep
> 1½ pound haddock, cod, or flounder fillets, cut into strips
> ¾ cup sifted all-purpose flour
> 1 teaspoon baking powder
> 1 teaspoon salt
> 1 egg, slightly beaten
> ½ cup milk
> 1 tablespoon melted butter

1. Add fat to pan. Heat to 380°.

2. As soon as proper temperature is reached (it will take 7-9 minutes), complete the frying of potatoes. Drain them between paper towels and place in hot oven to keep warm.

3. While potatoes are frying, cut fish into strips about 2 inches long. Dry between paper towels. Sift together flour, baking powder, and salt. Stir in egg, milk, and butter to make smooth batter. Dip fillets into batter, let excess drip off, then drop into hot fat. Fry until brown and crisp, drain on absorbent paper. Serve with chips. Cooking time: 13-20 minutes. Yield: 4-5 servings.

Fish Sticks

Heat 2 tablespoons oil in frypan set at 300°. Add 2 cloves garlic and 5 tablespoons chopped parsley. Put the frozen uncooked fish sticks into hot oil and brown on all sides. Cover, open vent and cook until fish sticks are done. Serves 3.

Flounder Au Vin

Wine, butter, mushrooms and onions are the magic ingredients here. They add a French touch to an essentially easy dish, to be served perhaps at a luncheon with noodles and buttered baby lima beans.

>   2 pounds flounder fillets
> Salt and pepper
>   4 tablespoons butter
> ½ cup white wine
> ½ cup chopped onions
>   1 cup canned sliced mushrooms
> ¼ cup mushroom liquid
> ½ teaspoon dried basil
>   1 egg
>   1 tablespoon lemon juice

1. Sprinkle fillets with salt and pepper.

2. Heat pan to 300°. Add butter, wine and onions. Stew until onions are tender (6 minutes). Add mushrooms, mushroom liquid, and basil, stir to blend, then put flounder on top of sauce. Cover pan, close vents and cook until fish is opaque. Time varies with thickness of the fillet, allow 6-10 minutes, but let fish be slightly underdone, rather than over since the cooking process continues even after fish is removed. Slide fillets onto hot serving platter.

3. Reduce heat to 180°. Beat egg with lemon juice, slowly stir in a spoonful of pan juice. (If pan seems dry, add more butter.) Return egg to pan. Let egg sauce heat for a minute, then spoon to top of fish and serve immediately. Cooking time: 15-18 minutes. Yield: 4-6 servings.

Fish à la Meuniere

This is a classic technique for cooking fish. The fish is dipped in flour and sautéed in butter (about ½ cup) in a skillet set at about 325°. When the fish is cooked on both sides, it is removed to a platter.

Lemon juice (about 2 tablespoons), finely chopped parsley (about 1 tablespoon), salt and pepper (about 1¼ teaspoons combined), are then quickly heated in the skillet in butter which remains from cooking the fish. The butter sauce is then poured over the fish waiting in the platter. Shelled shrimp and lobster, trout, flounder, sole and scallops all are amenable to this treatment.

Since butter cannot be heated at high temperatures, nor can cooking with butter continue for too long a period, *controlled* temperature such as the electric frypan provides is recommended for fish to be cooked *à la meuniere*.

Court Bouillon

In fine French cookery, a court bouillon is used as the stock for poaching and steaming fish. The procedure for making it is simplicity itself.

Combine in frypan 2 cups white wine, 4 cups water, 1 teaspoon salt, ¼ cup vinegar, ½ cup diced carrot, ½ cup diced onion, a bay leaf, and a sprinkling of thyme and parsley. Bring to boil at highest heat, then reduce to simmering temperature. Cover, close vent, and cook for half an hour. Strain or skim out vegetables with slotted spoon. Simmer large fish in cold court bouillon; simmer small fish in bouillon which has been brought to boiling first. Save in refrigerator for a few days to use in making sauces and fish soups, or freeze and use as needed.

Fillet of Flounder With Lobster Sauce

To make Fish Stock

In electric pan, combine 2 pounds raw fish bones and trimmings left from fish with 1 onion, a few sprigs parsley, 5 peppercorns, and a tablespoon butter. Add 2 cups water and 1 cup white wine. Season with salt. Bring to boil at highest temperature, then reduce heat and let simmer uncovered for 25 minutes. Strain and use as base for any sauce to be served with fish.

Rolled Flounder Fillets

Order 6 large fillets of flounder. Cut them in half and roll each one around a slim cooked carrot or half a large carrot trimmed to narrow size. Fasten with a toothpick. Place in electric pan and cover with fish stock, adding 1 cup milk to cover. Cook 10 minutes at simmering temperature, spooning hot liquid over the flounder rolls several times. Carefully remove the fish with a broad spatula and place on serving platter. Remove sauce to separate bowl. Remove toothpicks. Make Lobster Sauce.

Lobster Sauce

Melt 4 tablespoons butter in pan set at simmering point. Slowly stir in 4 tablespoons flour, 1 teaspoon grated onion or onion juice, 3 cups stock left from cooking flounder, and salt and pepper to taste. Cook until thickened, then stir in 1 cup hot cooked lobster which has been cut in pieces. Do not let the lobster boil after it has been added to the sauce. Pour hot over the fish rolls and serve. Six servings.

Fish Steaks With White Grapes

Salt and pepper 4 or 5 fish steaks (I like flounder), and set aside. Combine in pan 2 tablespoons butter, 2 teaspoons chopped fresh chives or onions, and 1 tablespoon flour. Set temperature at 225° or simmering point and let cook for a few minutes, then add 1 cup white wine and 1 cup condensed undiluted cream of mushroom soup. Stir until well blended, and *almost* boiling. Lay the steaks diagonally in the skillet matching their original form. Spoon sauce all over steaks. At the sides of the pan, lay blocks of chopped frozen spinach (10 ounces in all). Spread sauce over spinach, cover pan, close vents and cook for 10-12 minutes, or until fish steaks are done. Just before serving, add 1 cup seedless white grapes and let them heat quickly. This is a rather unorthodox combination of Fish Veronique and Fish Florentine, but it is delicious. A good ladies' luncheon dish.

Tuna Casserole

    1 13-ounce can tuna fish
    1 can button mushrooms
    1 can condensed undiluted cream of mushroom soup
    3 tablespoons light cream
    2 cups cooked fine noodles
    1 cup cooked peas

Drain the tuna fish. Flake it rather coarsely. Combine mushrooms, cream of mushroom soup, and cream, and fold into tuna. Grease a 9-inch ring mold with butter. Arrange layers of cooked noodles, tuna, a layer of peas, and mushroom mixture in mold. Sprinkle top with grated cheese. Set mold in skillet, pour in hot water about halfway, add a tablespoon of vinegar to prevent discoloration of pan and set temperature at 250°. Cover and cook until mold is firm. Serves 6.

Halibut and Oyster Ragout

The oyster sauce makes a real delicacy of any plain poached fish. However, I must warn you that if ever any food can be ruined by overcooking, it is the delicate oyster. Poach it only until the edges curl—no longer.

> 3 cups water
> 1 teaspoon lemon juice
> 1 small onion
> 2 stalks celery
> 6 halibut steaks
> 2½ cups oysters
> 4 tablespoons flour
> 4 tablespoons butter
> ½ teaspoon paprika
> ½ teaspoon salt
> 1 cup milk

1. Put water, lemon juice, onion and celery into electric pan. Bring to quick boil, then add halibut. Lower heat to simmer, and poach fish about 8 minutes until it is just done (the meat will be all white, no longer translucent). Discard vegetables but save the stock in which the fish cooked.

2. Poach oysters in their own liquor in pan set at 250°. When edges begin to curl, remove to platter. Add oyster liquor to liquid saved from cooking the halibut, and reduce to 1 cup by boiling quickly in pan set at highest point.

3. Make cream sauce by combining flour, butter, paprika and salt, then stirring slowly into fish liquors. Add milk and cook at 200°. When sauce is thick return halibut and oysters to pan long enough to heat. Garnish with tiny whole mushrooms. Serves 6.

Haddock and Mushrooms en Brochette

2 pounds haddock fillets
1½ teaspoons salt
1 teaspoon pepper
3 tablespoons olive oil or melted butter
1 egg, slightly beaten
3 tablespoons milk
¾ cup fine bread or cracker crumbs
1 pound fresh mushrooms, sliced ½″ thick
3 tablespoons fat for pan

1. Cut fillets into 1-inch squares. Combine salt, pepper and olive oil or butter, brush on fish, dip in combined egg and milk, then roll in crumbs. Let dry for a few minutes. String on skewers alternately with mushrooms (save stems for mushroom sauce or other recipes).

2. Heat pan to 380°. Add fat and as soon as it is hot, put in skewers and sauté until fish is tender, turning to brown all sides. Serve from pan with napkins wrapped around ring of skewer. Cooking time: 3-6 minutes. Yield: 4-6 servings.

Fish Dinner

4 potatoes, cut into balls with melon scoop
8 mushrooms
2 carrots, cut into slices
½ cup finely chopped celery
¼ cup finely chopped green onions
¼ cup butter
¼ cup water
1½ pounds fish steaks or fillets
Salt and pepper
Paprika

Arrange potatoes, carrots and whole mushrooms alternately around the edge of the pan as a border. Sprinkle celery and onions over vegetables, dot with butter and add water. Simmer, covered, for half an hour, then put fish in center of pan, spoon liquid from pan over it, season with salt, pepper and paprika, cover again and cook until done, about 10 or 15 minutes according to the size of the fish. Garnish with watercress or parsley.

Clam Newburg

Newburg recipes are frequently cooked at the table in a chafing dish. With the controlled heat such as the frypan provides, a double boiler (which is what the chafing dish really is) is not necessary even for the making of a Newburg sauce.

> 3 tablespoons butter
> 3 tablespoons flour
> ⅛ teaspoon cayenne pepper
> 1 cup heavy cream
> 1 cup undiluted evaporated milk
> Salt and pepper
> 1 teaspoon Worcestershire sauce
> 3 cups clams, cleaned and shucked
> ¼ cup sherry wine
> 4 egg yolks, beaten

Heat pan to 180°. Melt butter, blend in flour and cayenne. Add cream and evaporated milk, stirring constantly until smooth and creamy. Season with salt, pepper and Worcestershire sauce. Stir in clams, then add wine and egg yolks (stir some hot sauce into yolks, then pour into pan). Simmer (do not let boil) until clams are done. Serve over buttered toast points. Cooking time: About 20 minutes. Yield: 8 servings.

Maryland Crab Cakes

Buy canned crab meat or use 12 hard-shelled crabs for 2 cups meat.

2 cups flaked crab meat, fresh or canned
½ cup cracker meal
1 egg, slightly beaten
1½ teaspoons salt
¼ teaspoon pepper
Flour
3 tablespoons fat for pan

1. Combine all ingredients except flour and fat. Blend well. Shape into 8 cakes or patties. Chill if you have time. Roll in flour. Add fat to pan.

2. Heat to 370°, fry fish cakes until golden, turning once. Allow 2 for each serving. Good with potato salad or deep-fried potatoes. Cooking time: 6-10 minutes. Yield: 4 servings.

Fried Soft-Shell Crabs

Dip cleaned soft-shell crabs in flour seasoned with salt and pepper. Dip into egg diluted with 2 tablespoons milk or water. Roll in fine bread or cracker crumbs. Let crumbs dry. Fry in hot fat (heated to 370°).

Crab Stew

Frozen king crabs are new on the market. Thaw 2 6-ounce packages; remove cartilage and chop meat. Heat at simmering temperature with 2 cups undiluted evaporated milk, 2 cups fish or chicken stock, ½ cup light cream, dash of paprika and salt. Simmer for 10 minutes, serve in bowls with a dollop of butter and chopped chives.

Jubilee Clam Fritters

1½ cups cleaned clams
¼ cup clam liquor
1 egg, beaten slightly
¼ cup cream
1 cup all-purpose flour
2 teaspoons baking powder
1 teaspoon salt
⅛ teaspoon pepper
Fat for pan ½" deep

1. Put clams through food chopper or mince them. Add clam liquor, egg, and cream. Sift together flour, baking powder, salt and pepper. Combine with clam mixture to make smooth batter. Add fat to pan.

2. Heat pan to 380°. Drop batter by spoonfuls directly into hot fat, dipping spoon in hot fat each time. Drain on absorbent paper, garnish with sprigs of parsley, and serve very hot. Makes about 16 small fritters. Cooking time: 6-8 minutes. Yield: 4 servings.

Crab Meat au Sherry

Here is a recipe for the cook who likes "quick and easy" party food. This is fine for Saturday midnight supper.

Heat in skillet at 250° 3 cups flaked canned crab meat with 1 cup fine bread crumbs and 2 cups canned or home-made tomato sauce, 1 teaspoon lemon juice, 4 tablespoons of sherry and salt and pepper to taste. Keep warm in skillet until ready to serve, then stir in 3 tablespoons heavy cream. Serve right from the skillet over crisp toast with sections of lemons (their edges dipped in parsley). A good supper dish for eight.

Oyster Fry

Frozen or canned oysters "r" always in season, if you cannot buy them fresh. Just be sure they "r" not overcooked because I would sooner eat a piece of breaded Italian shoe leather.

> 1 quart (24 shucked) oysters, drained
> 1 cup fine bread or cracker crumbs
> 1 teaspoon salt
> ¼ teaspoon pepper
> 2 eggs, slightly beaten (for coating)
> 4 tablespoons butter
> 4-6 eggs, slightly beaten

1. Drain oysters thoroughly and dry between paper towels. Mix crumbs with salt and pepper. Dip oysters into eggs and seasoned crumbs. Repeat egg-crumb dipping. Let dry for a few minutes if possible so that crumbs will stick better.

2. Heat pan to 350°. Add half of butter, and as soon as it melts, put in oysters. Let them brown on both sides. Turn out oysters on hot platter. Add remainder of butter.

3. Reduce heat to 250°. Pour in eggs and cook until done but still creamy. Scramble eggs several times as they cook. Serve with oysters and sliced tomatoes. This recipe may be used for clams, scallops, shrimp, frog's legs, soft-shell crabs. Cooking time: 4-5 minutes. Four to six servings.

This is obviously a hearty dish which can be prepared with ease and alacrity, therefore it is perfection for a "short order" supper after a sporting event, a concert, etc. Just have everything ready beforehand and prepare it quickly and confidently at the table while the gang watches and waits.

Oyster Terrapin

A Sunday night supper dish which is an old-time favorite. It is good with a tossed green salad and cheese rolls, or corn bread made from the recipe on the package of Quaker yellow cornmeal.

> 2 quarts oysters
> 4 cups heavy cream
> 1 cup chicken stock or milk
> 1 cup sliced mushrooms
> ½ cup butter
> 1 cup flour
> 4 hard-cooked eggs, diced
> Salt and fresh pepper
> Dash of mustard and cayenne
> 2 teaspoons celery salt
> 1 tablespoon grated onion or onion juice
> 2 teaspoons Worcestershire sauce
> ¼ cup dry sherry

Poach oysters in their own liquor in skillet set at 250°. When edges curl, remove from pan and drain dry. Add remaining ingredients except sherry and cook for 15 minutes until sauce thickens. Add cooked oysters and sherry and serve as soon as heated in individual casseroles. Serves 8.

Oysters in Blankets

Wrap oysters in a piece of bacon; hold with toothpick; pan-broil in cold frypan set at 340°. Turn and cook until bacon is crisp. Allow 4 per serving. Also makes a fine hors d'oeuvre.

Sautéed Scallops

The bay scallops are sweeter; if they are not available cut the large sea scallops in half before you sauté them.

> 2 pounds bay scallops (about 1 quart)
> ¼ cup milk
> 1 clove garlic, peeled and crushed
> Salt and pepper
> 1 egg slightly beaten with 2 tablespoons cold water
> ¾ cup fine bread crumbs
> 4 tablespoons butter

1. Wash and dry scallops. Combine milk, garlic, salt and pepper. Pour over scallops and let stand for at least ten or 15 minutes. Drain, dry, dip in eggs and roll in crumbs. Let dry.

2. Heat butter in pan set at 325°, brown scallops on both sides. Turn out on absorbent paper to dry. Serve with Quick Tartar Sauce. Cooking time: 5-8 minutes. Yield: 6-8 servings. Scallops are also good served *à la meuniere*, see page 59.

Quick Tartar Sauce

To 1 cup mayonnaise, add as many of the following ingredients as possible, making a total of ¾ cup: grated onion, finely cut olives, shredded pimentos, diced parsley, chopped pickle or cucumber, chopped celery, chopped capers. Blend well.

Note: Pan-fried oysters are excellent this way. Melt 3 tablespoons butter in pan at 360°, add ¼ cup finely chopped celery, cook 4 minutes until soft, then add 2 dozen large oysters. As soon as edges curl up, pour in ¼ cup sherry. Heat. Season with salt and pepper, serve over crisp toast. Yield: 4 servings.

Shrimp Fra Diavolo in Rice Ring

A spicy deviled shrimp dish; it can be cooked ahead and kept warm for a short period but do not overcook or shrimps will toughen.

>   3 pounds uncooked shrimps
>   4 tablespoons cooking oil
>   ½ cup chopped onion
>   2 cloves garlic, minced or crushed fine
>   3½ cups stewed tomatoes canned
>   1 teaspoon salt
>   ½ teaspoon paprika
>   Pinch of cayenne
>   2 teaspoons oregano
>   1 teaspoon lemon juice
>   2 tablespoons cornstarch
>   2 tablespoons water

Clean shrimps, removing shells and veins but do not cook them. Set skillet at 250°, heat oil and when light signal goes off, add shrimp, onion and garlic. Cook at low heat, stirring frequently. When shrimps look opaque and pink, add tomatoes, salt, paprika, cayenne, oregano and lemon juice and continue cooking for about 15 minutes. Smooth out cornstarch in water, then stir into skillet. Continue cooking until sauce is thick. For attractive buffet service, pack 6 cups hot cooked and buttered rice into a 9-inch ring mold and invert into skillet. Serves 6.

Shrimp Diavolo Flambé

Pour 2 tablespoons brandy into the shrimp in skillet. Warm 2 tablespoons brandy in a separate saucepan or butter melter, light it and pour over shrimp to serve.

Steamed Shrimp

Wash the shrimps in several waters. Put on a rack in electric pan. (I use a rack which came with a small broiler.) Pour in boiling water only to top of the rack. Add a sprig or two of fresh dill. Cover and boil for two minutes at 350°. Turn off heat and let shrimp steam, with cover on, for 2 minutes more. Remove from rack. When shrimp is cool enough to handle, remove shell and intestinal vein. Use as desired. Steaming is the best way to cook fish to retain its flavor and food values.

A good cocktail sauce for shrimp: Combine ½ cup chili sauce, 1 tablespoon horseradish sauce, 2 teaspoons lemon juice, 2 teaspoons Worcestershire sauce, and a dash of Tabasco sauce.

Scampi Marinara

Translated, this is Shrimp Mariners' Style

 ¼ cup olive oil
 3 garlic cloves, minced or crushed fine
 2½ cups canned Italian tomatoes
 ⅓ cup Italian tomato paste
 ½ teaspoon basil
 2½ teaspoons salt
   Pinch of red pepper
 1 teaspoon oregano
 2 pounds large shrimps, cooked and cleaned

Heat oil in skillet at 300°, brown garlic and remove large pieces. Add tomatoes, tomato paste, basil, salt, pepper and oregano. Cover and simmer for 1 hour. Stir in shrimp, heat and serve with breadsticks. Good over buttered cooked spaghetti, with endive salad and Roquefort cheese dressing. Serves 4 to 6.

Shrimps With Green Peas and Rice

This is a lovely party dish—midnight supper variety—because it is easy to do, delicious, and universally popular.

1½ cups long grain rice
1 package frozen peas
3 tablespoons butter
2 pounds shrimp, cleaned and cooked
Salt and pepper
½ cup dry sherry
1½ cups cream, thick
3 egg yolks
½ cup light cream

Cook rice as directed on package at 300° Do not stir it or remove cover except toward the end to see if rice is almost soft. When it is not quite done, add the peas which have been somewhat defrosted and toss them together with a wooden spoon. Push them to sides of the pan. Reduce heat to 200°. In the center of the pan melt butter, toss in shrimp, add sherry and heavy cream and stir together. Heat for a few minutes. Mix egg yolks with light cream and stir into dish. Season to taste with salt and pepper. Serve shrimp, rice and sauce in each plate. Serves 6.

French Fried Shrimp

Shell and devein shrimp, leaving tails on. Dip in flour, beaten egg and finally in seasoned bread crumbs. Heat oil in frypan set at 360° (oil should be about ⅓ of the way up). When light goes off, fry shrimp 3 to 5 minutes, depending on size. Serve golden brown on both sides.

Tempura (Illustrated in color on the jacket)

Raw medium shrimp
Striped bass
Zucchini squash
Eggplant
Whole green beans
Asparagus tips
Leeks
Spinach leaves
Parsley
Cornstarch, for dusting
Tempura Batter
Corn oil for frying (about 1¼ cups)

Shell and clean shrimp. Cut striped bass into finger-size pieces. Cut squash and eggplant into pencil-thin strips. Trim ends from green beans. If leeks are large, cut off tops leaving some of the green; slice lengthwise. Wash and dry spinach leaves and parsley. Dust pieces of fish and vegetables lightly but evenly with cornstarch; dip into Tempura Batter; drain on wire racks. Meanwhile, heat corn oil in frypan to 375°F. Oil should be a scant 1 inch deep, but should not fill skillet-frypan more than ⅓ full. Fry food, turning to cook both sides; it will brown only very delicately during cooking. Drain on absorbent paper. Serve immediately with soy sauce.

Tempura Batter: Sift ¼ cup cornstarch and ¾ cup flour together. Stir in 1 cup water, then 1 egg. Beat with rotary beater until well blended. Enough batter for about 4 servings.

Shrimp Jambalaya

    4 tablespoons butter or olive oil
    ½ cup diced ham
    ½ cup diced onions
    ¼ cup diced green peppers
    ¼ cup diced celery
    1 clove garlic, diced
    1 cup raw rice
    ¼ teaspoon Spanish saffron
    1 teaspoon salt
    1½ pounds raw shrimp, cleaned and veined

Heat pan to 350°. Melt butter, and put in ham, onions, green peppers, celery and garlic. Cook until onions are tender, stirring frequently. Pour in 2 cups water and let boil. Now add rice, tomatoes, saffron and salt. Cover and bring to boil, then reduce heat to simmering. Continue cooking until rice is almost done, then add shrimp and cook 10 minutes longer. Cooking time: 30-40 minutes. Yield: 6-8 servings.

Lobster Newburg

In pan set at 275° combine 4 tablespoons butter, ½ teaspoon paprika, a dash of Tabasco sauce, and ½ cup sherry or madeira wine. Cook for about 10 minutes or until most of wine is cooked away. Reduce temperature to simmering point.

Stir together 1½ cups cream and 4 beaten egg yolks, pour a tablespoon of sauce from frypan into cream and egg mixture, then return mixture to pan. Let simmer for 10 minutes more, then add 1 tablespoon cognac. Stir in 2 cups diced cooked lobster meat and heat for 5 minutes but do not let it boil. Serve on freshly buttered toast with a dash of paprika. If you have lobster coral or the lobster shell, use as garnish.

Lobster Cantonese

This may not be an authentic Chinese recipe, but it is as completely gratifying in texture and taste as those which bear the imprint of a fine Oriental hand.

> 3 packages frozen lobster tails
> 1 pound lean pork, ground coarsely
> 3 tablespoons oil
> 1½ teaspoons salt
> Dash of pepper
> 2 tablespoons finely chopped water chestnuts
> 2 teaspoons finely chopped green onions
> 1½ cups chicken stock or bouillon
> 2 eggs
> 3 tablespoons cornstarch
> 1 tablespoon soy sauce
> ⅓ cup water

Cover lobster tails with salted cold water in skillet. Heat to 250°. When light goes off, lobster tails are ready. Remove them from skillet. Save water in which they cooked. Cool, then remove meat from shells and cut into large dice. Save shells. Heat oil to 350°, when light signal goes off, add pork, salt and pepper, water chestnuts, and scallions. Cook 15 minutes, stirring frequently. To skillet, add bouillon and water in which lobsters cooked. Cook about 10 minutes longer. Lower heat to simmering. Stir in the eggs. Cook for a few minutes. Combine cornstarch, soy sauce and water. Add gradually to skillet and cook until sauce is thickened. Add cut-up lobster tails before serving and let get real hot. Serve over boiled rice. Hang shells over sides of serving dish or skillet as decoration. 6 servings.

Lobster Margarita (Langosta Flambee Margarita)

"A lobster dish with an incomparable flare and fillip to the Venezuelan sauce that will earn for any woman the distinction of being the 'hostess with the mostest'. We think you'll agree that any descriptive adjectives would only be superfluous and could not really begin to do justice to the wonderful succulence of this dish." So runs the comment which accompanies this recipe developed by the Creole Petroleum Corporation, to whom we are indebted for its use.

4 packages frozen lobster tails
¼ cup butter or margarine
½ onion, minced
1 clove garlic, crushed
½ teaspoon salt
¼ teaspoon pepper
¼ teaspoon oregano
¼ teaspoon nutmeg
¼ cup flour
¾ cup canned beef consommé
½ cup apple juice or cider
Juice of ½ lemon
Dash of Angostura bitters
2 tablespoons chopped parsley
2 egg yolks
3 cups cooked rice
¼ cup rum
Parsley sprigs to garnish

1. Put lobster tails in cold water which has been salted. Heat at 300° until water comes to boil, at which time lobster tails are done.

2. Meanwhile, melt half of the butter or margarine in the pan and sauté in it chopped onion and garlic until tender. Add remaining butter and seasonings. Blend in flour. Now stir

in beef consommé, apple juice, lemon juice and bitters and heat. Stir constantly until thickened and smooth. Add chopped parsley.

3. Lightly beat egg yolks with a fork, add a little of the heated sauce to the yolks, and then stir them back into the sauce. Simmer, stirring for 2 or 3 minutes.

4. Rinse lobster tails, remove from shell and cut in half crosswise. On a large round platter, make a wreath of hot cooked rice; fill center with lobster.

5. In a small skillet or butter melter, heat ¼ cup rum. Carefully ignite at table. Meanwhile quickly top lobster with hot sauce and pour burning rum over all. Garnish with parsley sprigs and serve at once. Serves 6.

Shrimp and Lobster Patties

These patties would make a good luncheon dish but do not serve too strong a sauce or you will disguise their delicate flavor.

1 cup cooked cleaned shrimp and lobster
Few sprigs of dill
2 slices day-old bread
2 tablespoons butter
Salt and pepper
4 tablespoons fat for skillet

Put the shrimp, lobster and dill through the fine blade of a meat grinder. (Tuck the herb in first to be sure it goes through). Soak the bread in water, squeeze it dry and mix with sea food. Add butter, salt and pepper. Shape mixture into patties. Just before serving, heat fat in skillet set at 350°. When hot, brown patties on both sides. Serve with medium white sauce (fresh chopped dill is a good addition) and green salad for a luncheon or midnight supper. Serves 4-5.

Scalloped Salmon

In frypan set at 300°, cook gently (do not brown) in 2 table-spoons fat, ½ cup minced onion, 3 tablespoons minced green pepper, and 2 tablespoons minced celery. Reduce heat to simmering temperature. Add 2 No. 2 cans of salmon, 1 teaspoon Worcestershire sauce, 3 cups mashed potatoes, 1 cup milk, 1 teaspoon salt, a dash of pepper and 2 tablespoons finely minced parsley. Cook 20 minutes. Serve on toast. Two cups of cooked peas can be stirred in at the last, and allowed to heat. Serves 10.

MEATS, PLAIN
AND FANCY

53 RECIPES

Recipes in This Chapter

Beef and Variety Meats

Steak Au Poivre, 81
Rolled Steak Wheels, 82
Chinese Pepper Steak, 82
Beef Filet Stroganov, 83
Suki-Yaki, 84
Beef, Olive and Potato Ragout, 86
Pot Roast with Gingersnap
    Gravy, 87
Hash from Leftover Pot Roast, 87
Savory Beef Stew and
    Vegetables, 88
Meat Loaf Ring, 88
Skillet Meat Loaf Casserole, 89
Hamburger Mixed Grill, 89
Swedish Meat Balls, 90
Shepherd's Pies, 90
Italian Meat Balls in
    Spaghetti Sauce, 91
Beef-Stuffed Pimentos, 92
Chicken Livers with Fried
    Apple Rings, 93
Liver and Mushroom Skewers, 93
Calves Liver Sautéed in Wine, 94
Sweet and Sour Tongue, 94
Sweetbreads and Mushrooms, 95
Sautéed Brains, 95

Veal

Breaded Veal, 96
Veal Scallopini, 96
Veal Parmigiana, 96
Veal Mozzarella, 96
Veal Milanese, 97

Wiener Schnitzel, 97
Schnitzel à la Holstein, 97
Saltimbocca, 97
Veal Chops with Herbs, 98
Veal Stew, 98
Veal Casserole, 99

Lamb

Lamb Chops in Burgundy, 99
Breaded Lamb Cutlets, 100
Pan-Broiled Lamb Chops, 100
Roquefort Chops, 100
Patlijian, 101
Turkish Lamb Rolls, 101
Lamb Stew, 102
Dumplings, 102

Ham, Bacon, Pork, Sausages

Ham and Potato Skillet, 103
Ham, Egg and Banana Grill, 103
Pan-Broiled Bacon, 103
Pineapple Hamburgers, 104
Sausages, 104
Savory Frankfurter and
    Cabbage, 105
Frankfurter and Bean
    Casserole, 105
Sweet Cherries and Pork
    Chops, 106
Pork Chop Casserole, 106
Cantonese Spareribs, 107
Sausage and Baked Bean
    Casserole, 107
Barbecued Spareribs, 108

Steak au Poivre

This is a good company dish to cook at the table. The first course—chilled vichyssoise or madrilene—can be served and waiting for guests before they come to dinner.

> 3 to 4-pound sirloin steak, about 1" thick
> Kitchen Bouquet
> 2 tablespoons flour
> 2 tablespoons crushed black peppercorns
> 3 tablespoons combined butter and olive oil
> 3 tablespoons cognac
> ¼ cup white wine

1. *In advance:* Be sure the steak fits your skillet. If not, trim it to proper size. Remove fat from edges and brush meat on both sides with Kitchen Bouquet. Sprinkle with flour. Press crushed pepper into both sides. Refrigerate until ready to use.

2. *15 minutes before serving:* Heat butter and oil in skillet set at 300°, add steak and brown on both sides, allowing 8 to 10 minutes total for medium rare.

3. When steak is as you like it, move it to a large platter; add cognac and wine to fat in pan. Stir, being certain to pick up the pieces which cling to the bottom of the pan.

4. While the sauce cooks (5 minutes in all) cut the steak into diagonal pieces and serve promptly with hot sauce mixed with steak juices. For those non-gourmets who prefer well-done steak, put some cut pieces back into skillet to cook with sauce. Not as good, but they probably won't know the difference!

Plate Dinner: Steak au Poivre. Shoestring Potatoes (recipe on page 146). Fry them ahead and keep warm in 250° oven. Tomatoes Provençale, page 154. Transfer to shallow casserole and keep in warm oven.

Rolled Steak Wheels

2 pounds shoulder beef steak sliced ¼" thick
Salt and pepper
½ cup shelled green peas
½ cup finely diced carrots
½ cup diced celery including the very young leaves
1 tablespoon fresh parsley sprigs, cut fine
Paprika
3 tablespoons olive oil
2 large sweet onions

Pound the shoulder steaks thin (a heavy can will do it) and season them with salt and pepper. Combine the peas, carrots, celery and parsley and spread over the steak roll. Secure with toothpicks. Sprinkle with paprika and brown in hot olive oil in skillet set at 350°. Cut the onions into slices and put over the meat, add ½ cup hot water, cover, close vents and simmer for an hour and a half or until beef is done. When ready to serve cut into wheels 2" thick. Serve with gravy over kasha or mashed potatoes. Looks pretty and is very good. Serves 6.

Chinese Pepper Steak

1½ pounds flank steak
3 tablespoons soy sauce
1 tablespoon sherry wine
½ teaspoon sugar
1 teaspoon cornstarch
½ teaspoon salt
3 green peppers
3 tablespoons oil
Potato chips

Cut flank steak across grain and diagonally into strips ⅛" x 4" x 1". Pound lightly with a knife. Combine soy sauce, sherry, sugar, cornstarch and salt and spread over meat. Let stand until ready to cook.

Cut seeded green peppers into strips 1" wide. Heat oil at 350° and when oil is hot, add green pepper strips. Cook 3 minutes, turning occasionally. Push vegetable to sides of pan and add meat. Cook 2 minutes more. The meat should be rare, and the green pepper crisp. Arrange a border of fresh potato chips around the skillet (or whatever serving dish you are using) and serve hot. Serves 6.

Beef Filet Stroganov

(Recipe by Michael Mozer, Chef, Russian Bear Restaurant in New York)

1. Cut a three-pound fillet of beef into pieces the size of ladyfingers.

2. Slice 6 onions Julienne and fry in ½ pound butter in skillet set at 300° for a few minutes. Add the beef to the skillet, mix with onions and let cook gently until done as you like it. Do not overcook, this cut of beef is best when it is served rare.

3. Add 1 pound sliced mushrooms which have first been cooked in water, salt, pepper, 3 tablespoons flour, and a dash of A-1 sauce and ketchup.

4. Stir in 1 cup sour cream and mix thoroughly on low heat. Heavy cream or evaporated milk will make the sauce finer and more plentiful. Serves 8.

Suki-yaki

Bernard Wile, gourmet, author of Cooking For One And Two, *contributes this recipe. He says "Here is a dish with which you can put on a display of culinary virtuosity to impress your guests, not only with your familiarity with exotic viands, but with your casual deftness in the handling of foods, for suki-yaki should be cooked at the table. A certain amount of preparation can be done in advance, namely getting the ingredients into shape to toss into the pot. In so doing, you can get a colorful and appetizing platter to bring to the table."*

> 2 ounces beef suet
> 1 pound round steak
> 2 large Bermuda onions
> 16 fresh mushrooms
> 1 cup white wine
> 1 cup chicken broth
> ½ cup soya sauce
> 2 teaspoons sugar
> 6 water chestnuts
> ½ can bean sprouts
> 4 tablespoons bamboo shoots
> 1 pound leaf spinach

Have the steak cut into ⅛-inch thick slices, pound between two pieces of Saran-wrap to make it even thinner and cut it into strips about 1 inch wide and 4 inches long. Lay these at one end of a large serving platter, the strips overlapping. Peel the onion and slice it into ¼-inch thick slices and lay these at the other end of the platter. Slice the mushrooms into three pieces lengthwise. Add these to the platter. Slice the water chestnuts thinly and add them. (You may substitute a rib of celery cut into ½ inch chunks.) Also lay out the bamboo shoots and the bean sprouts. Wash the spinach well and place it in the center of your platter. Set the cube of beef suet at the edge where you can find it. The wine and chicken broth can be in cruets or small pitchers at the table, the soya sauce can be served in its own bottle. The sugar can be in a bowl.

Heat the skillet to 380°. When hot, rub the surface with the suet and leave the cube in. Lay in the strips of beef and brown them on both sides, then add the onions and the mushrooms and let them fry with the beef for about 4 or 5 minutes. Then add all the rest of the ingredients except the spinach and let cook for about ten minutes, stirring once in a while. Next, add the spinach, cover the pan and let the greens steam for three minutes, no more. Uncover and serve over hot rice which you will have prepared. For a beverage, have a large pot of hot tea. Serves 4.

With this dinner, you can, of course serve hot Saki. We don't believe that it will be missed if you do not serve it. Serves 4.

Menu: *Sashimi*—Cut as thin as possible ¼ pound boneless thick fillet of *fresh* haddock, flounder, halibut or tuna. Cover with juice of 2 lemons, equal amount of soy sauce. Marinate for an hour or so. This is the hors d'oeuvre. Don't turn up your nose until you've tasted it.

Shrimp Tempura, recipe on page 73
Cooked Rice   *Suki-Yaki*
Hot Tea

(Dessert is neither traditional nor needed. If you must, try fresh fruit or canned pineapple wtih cookies. Pineapple garnished with kumquats (recipe page 188) is also suitable.)

Beef, Olive and Potato Ragout

Stew of course, but doesn't it taste better under a company name?

> 2 pounds beef cut into 1-inch pieces
> 3 tablespoons grated lemon rind
> ¼ cup flour
> 2 teaspoons salt
> ¼ teaspoon pepper
> Dash of nutmeg
> 3 tablespoons oil
> 2 cloves garlic
> 1 cup canned tomatoes
> 2 cups beef stock or bouillon
> 1 teaspoon chopped parsley
> ½ teaspoon dried thyme
> 1 bay leaf
> 6 small potatoes, quartered
> ½ cup pitted olives.

1. Wipe beef. In a paper bag, combine lemon rind, flour, salt, pepper, nutmeg, and a few pieces of beef. Shake until beef is well coated. Repeat.

2. Heat pan to 340°. When light blinks off, add oil. Heat to sizzling, brown floured beef and garlic on all sides. Discard garlic. Pour in tomatoes, stock, parsley, thyme, and bay leaf. As soon as boiling point is reached (in a minute or two).

3. Reduce heat to simmering temperature. Cover and stew for 2 hours. Now add potatoes in a border around pan, sprinkle with olives, and continue cooking until beef is tender. Cooking time: 2½-3 hours. Yield: 6 servings.

Pot Roast with Gingersnap Gravy

1 cup vinegar
1 cup water
1 bay leaf
4 peppercorns
1 small onion, diced
Dash of mace
2 whole cloves
1 clove garlic, mashed
3- 5-pound pot roast
3 tablespoons flour
2 tablespoons cold water
½ cup fine gingersnap crumbs

1. Combine vinegar, water, bay leaf, peppercorns, onion, mace, cloves, and garlic to make a marinade sauce. Pour over pot roast and let stand in refrigerator for 1 day, turning several times. Remove beef, drain (save marinade) and dry. Sprinkle with flour.

2. Heat pan to 300°. Brown roast on all sides. Add marinade sauce. Cover pan, close vent.

3. Lower heat to simmering temperature. Let simmer (not boil) until tender, turning several times so all sides keep moist. Remove to platter. Stir gingersnaps into pan, heat, and serve immediately. Cooking time: 2½ hours. Yield: 6-8 servings.

Hash from Leftover Pot Roast

Mince fine or put through grinder 2 cups leftover cooked beef with 1 cup cooked potatoes. Sauté 1 small diced onion in 2 tablespoons fat in frypan set at 300°. When soft add beef and potatoes with 3 tablespoons milk. Heat, taste to correct seasoning. Serves 4-6.

Savory Beef Stew and Vegetables

8 slices bacon
3 medium onions, chopped
2 pounds beef, cut into chunks
2 teaspoons salt
½ teaspoon pepper
1½ cups red wine (or beef stock)
6 large potatoes, pared and quartered
3 medium turnips, pared and quartered
6 carrots, scrubbed
2 cups sour cream

1. Heat pan to 350°. Cut each bacon slice into 4 pieces. Brown in pan. Add onions and cook until soft. Brown beef on all sides. Add salt, pepper, and wine, and bring to boil.
2. Reduce heat to simmering temperature. Cover, close vent, and continue cooking for 1½ hours. Add potatoes, turnips, and carrots, and let simmer until vegetables are almost tender. Stir in sour cream, and continue cooking 10 minutes longer. Cooking time: 2¼ hours. Yield: 6 servings.

To hold dinner: This beef stew improves while waiting. Just be sure there is enough liquid, and do not add sour cream until you are ready to eat.

Meat Loaf Ring

Combine 3 pounds of hamburger, 2 eggs slightly beaten, 2 teaspoons salt, dash of pepper, a mashed clove of garlic, ½ cup grated onion, with 1 cup cornflakes. Blend well. Put into 9″ ring mold. Spoon over it ½ cup canned tomato sauce. Set mold into skillet in about an inch of water. Cover pan and cook at 325° for 1½ hours. Turn meat loaf out of mold and fill center with buttered cooked noodles, with a ring of baby beets around the outside and fringes of parsley between the beets. Serves 8-10.

Skillet Meat Loaf Casserole

1 pound chopped beafsteak
1 egg, slightly beaten
1 cup soft bread crumbs
¼ cup tomato sauce or ketchup
1 teaspoon Worcestershire sauce
1 teaspoon salt
¼ teaspoon pepper
¼ cup flour
1 tablespoon fat
¼ cup beef stock or bouillon
8 small potatoes
2 zucchini, cut into strips
1 teaspoon grated onion

Combine the beefsteak, egg, bread, tomato sauce, Worcestershire, salt and pepper; form into a compact loaf to fit the middle of your skillet. Dredge in flour.

Heat pan to 300°. Add fat and as soon as it is heated, put in loaf, and brown it on all sides. Add bouillon, cover pan, and simmer 15 minutes. Put in potatoes, cover again, and cook about half an hour longer until potatoes are just about tender, then tuck zucchini around the pan, sprinkle with onion, cover and simmer 15 minutes longer until tender. Cooking time: About 1 hour. Yield: 4 servings.

Hamburger Mixed Grill

Melt 3 tablespoons fat in preheated pan set at 350°. Tilt pan to spread fat. Put hamburger patties into pan surrounded by slices of mushrooms and thick slices of tomato which have been dipped in seasoned bread crumbs. Canned chili beans may be heated in corners of pan. Turn everything once. Allow 8 minutes for a 1″ thick hamburger. For thicker burgers, close pan, reduce heat to 300° and cook until done as you like.

Swedish Meat Balls

¾ pound beef
½ pound pork
¼ pound veal
1 cup soft, coarse bread crumbs
½ cup milk
1 egg, slightly beaten
3 tablespoons onion juice
1 teaspoon salt
¼ teaspoon pepper
2 tablespoons butter or oil for pan

Grind beef, pork, and veal together twice. Add other ingredients, except butter or oil, and blend well. With a teaspoon, shape the mixture into tiny balls. Heat pan to 375°. Add butter or oil, brown meat balls on all sides. Serve hot. Cooking time: 8-10 minutes. Yield: 6 servings.

Shepherd's Pies

2 pounds ground beef
1 tablespoon grated onion
2 cups seasoned mashed potatoes
1 egg, beaten
1 tablespoon lemon or lime juice
Fine bread crumbs
3 tablespoons fat or cooking oil

1. Combine beef and onion. Shape into patties. Press potatoes around patties. Dilute egg with lemon juice. Dip patties into egg, then cover with crumbs. Repeat egg and crumbs.

2. Heat pan to 360°. Melt fat. Put in patties and brown on both sides, turning once with a pancake turner. Serve hot. Cooking time: 12-15 minutes. Yield: 6 servings.

Italian Meat Balls in Spaghetti Sauce

This is a real Italian sauce, not an insipid imitation.

1½ pounds ground beef
3 tablespoons flour
2 tablespoons fat or oil
1 pound boned loin of pork, cut into chunks
3 cloves garlic, mashed
1 can (No. 2½) red pack tomatoes
1 small can Italian tomato paste
1 teaspoon salt
Dash of red pepper
Dash of black pepper
1 pound sweet Italian sausages

1. Shape beef into 18 balls. Roll in flour. Heat pan to 300°.

2. Heat fat, add meat balls, pork, and garlic, and brown on all sides. Transfer to platter. Prick sausages with fork, put into pan with ½ cup water, cook for 5 minutes. Drain. Remove to platter.

3. Pour tomatoes and tomato paste into pan. Fill tomato paste can with water, and add to pan. As soon as liquid boils, put meat balls, sausages, and pork back into pan. Add seasonings.

4. Reduce heat to simmering temperature—liquid boils gently when light is on. Cover and cook for 2 hours. Skim off fat. If sauce is too thick, add hot water. Serve over cooked spaghetti, macaroni, or noodles. Grated Parmesan cheese is essential of course. Cooking time: 2 hours. Yield: 6 servings.

Dividend Cooking: Triple or quadruple this recipe (except for the spaghetti which does not freeze well). Freeze surplus in quart-size containers. To serve, remove frozen block from container. Heat ½ cup beef stock, tomato sauce or water in skillet, add frozen sauce and heat, covered and vent closed, at simmering temperature.

Beef-Stuffed Pimentos

  2 tablespoons butter or margarine
  1 small onion, finely chopped
  ¾ pound ground beefsteak
  2 cans (4-ounces each) whole pimentos
  ½ cup sifted all-purpose flour
  1 teaspoon salt
  ½ teaspoon baking powder
  1 egg
  ¼ cup milk
  Oil for pan ⅓ full

Heat pan to 350°. Add butter or margarine, and as soon as it melts, cook onion until soft. Add beefsteak, and let it brown. Spoon beef into pimentos, handling pimentos carefully so they do not split. Combine flour, salt, baking powder, egg, and milk to make batter. Mix until smooth. Carefully slide stuffed pimentos into batter, then let excess drain off. Add oil to washed preheated pan.

Heat to 380°. Now transfer pimentos to hot fat, and let fry until brown on all sides. Dry on absorbent paper. Serve hot. Cooking time: 2-3 minutes. Yield: 4 servings.

Note: Lamb hash is another good stuffing for pimentos. To make it combine ¾ cup finely diced cooked lamb, 2 tablespoons green pepper, chopped and sautéed in butter, ¼ cup cooked diced potatoes, 3 tablespoons leftover gravy, tomato sauce, salt and pepper to taste.

Freezer Note: Stuffed pimentos may be frozen one layer deep (a foil plate is fine) wrapped in freezer bags and simmered for 8 to 10 minutes in a rich tomato sauce when ready to serve.

Chicken Livers with Fried Apple Rings

1 pound chicken livers
Flour seasoned with salt and pepper
3 tablespoons butter
8 peeled and cored tart apple rings
½ cup sliced shallots, scallions or onions

Cut the livers in half, wash and dry them, then roll in flour which has been seasoned with salt and pepper. Melt butter in skillet set at 275°, dip the apple rings in the butter, then move them to the sides of the pan. Cook the shallots and livers in the center of frypan. Serve with buttered rice as a luncheon dish or with scrambled eggs for a hearty brunch. Tiny sausages may be cooked first then tucked into the centers of the apple rings, or green mint jelly may be used to fill centers. Serves 4.

Liver and Mushroom Skewers

1 pound liver, sliced ½-inch thick
1 cup large mushroom caps
¼ cup flour
Salt and pepper
4 tablespoons fat for pan
4 thick slices tomato, well seasoned

Wipe liver. Remove membrane and veins. Cut into 1½-inch squares. Wipe mushrooms. Put flour, salt and pepper in paper bag. Shake liver and mushrooms, a few pieces at a time, in bag. When coated well, arrange alternately on skewers. (Skewer the liver through the ½-inch side.)

Heat pan with oil or butter to 350° when light goes off, add skewers and brown on both sides. Serve with thick tomato slices. Cooking time: 2-4 minutes. Yield: 4 servings.

Calves Liver Sautéed in Wine

12 slices bacon
6 slices calves liver, ¼" thick
¼ cup seasoned flour
3 tablespoons butter
1 tablespoon minced scallion
½ cup dry red wine

Fry bacon in cold skillet at 320° until crisp. Take out slices as they brown and drain on paper towels. Sprinkle liver with flour which has been seasoned with salt and pepper. Remove all but a thin film of bacon fat from skillet, add liver and sauté at 320°, turning once. Push to sides of pan. Melt butter in middle of the skillet and cook scallions for a few minutes. Remove liver to hot platter, add wine and cook, stirring up all the bits and pieces which are clinging to the skillet. Pour sauce over liver when very hot and serve with bacon. 6 servings. Garnish with parsley and tomato wedges marinated in French dressing. Hash brown potatoes (see page 147) can be cooked in skillet as soon as liver is done.

Sweet and Sour Tongue

1 boiled beef tongue, cooked slightly underdone
4 gingersnaps
½ cup brown sugar
½ cup vinegar
1 teaspoon grated onion
1 cup hot water
1 lemon, sliced
½ cup almonds, skin removed
¼ cup raisins

Slice the tongue. In frypan, set at 300°, cook together until smooth, the gingersnaps, brown sugar, vinegar, onion juice and hot water. Stir to mix, then add lemon, raisins, almonds and tongue and simmer at about 225° for another half hour. Taste for seasoning and add vinegar or sugar. Serves 8 as first course; or 6 as main dish.

Sweetbreads and Mushrooms

1. Cover 2 pairs of sweetbreads with cold water, 1 teaspoon salt and 1 tablespoon vinegar. Parboil for 20 minutes. Drain, chill and cut into 1-inch cubes, discarding any tissue.

2. Melt 2 tablespoons butter in electric pan set at 225°, brown sweetbreads and move to sides of pan. Add and brown 1 pound sliced mushrooms, and also move to sides of pan.

3. Add 3 tablespoons butter, melt, stir in 4 tablespoons flour and 1½ cups cream. Let come to slow boil. Stir in 2 tablespoons wine.

4. Bring everything to slow boil, stirring well together. Serve in a ring of wild rice, made according to package directions. Surround wild rice with cooked and buttered lima beans. Serves 6. An outstanding luncheon dish.

Sautéed Brains

Brains are an edible food which according to Escoffier "form a wholesome and rebuilding diet for all who are weakened by excessive head-work"! He recommends that they be cleaned, membranes removed, put into boiling court bouillon (page 59) to cover, skimmed, then simmered for half an hour. Brains may be substituted for sweetbreads or used in combination with them in the preceding recipe, or for that matter in any other recipe.

Breaded Veal

Get veal slices cut very thin (as for scallopini). Flatten them further by beating with a meat mallet or the side of a heavy can, to break down any tough fibers.

1. Prepare 3 large dishes. Put flour seasoned with salt and pepper into the first dish. Put a beaten egg mixed with 2 tablespoons of water (and a dash of Worcestershire sauce perhaps) into the second dish. Put fine bread crumbs into the third dish. Dip the veal in each of the three dishes, in the order listed.

2. Heat ¼ cup olive oil and butter combination (or use all cooking oil) in pan set at 350°. When hot, add veal and cook on both sides until evenly well browned. A pound of veal will serve 3 or 4.

Veal Scallopini

Follow recipe for Breaded Veal. Combine 1 tablespoon lemon juice and 1 cup white wine. Heat quickly in skillet, pour over browned veal.

Veal Parmigiana

Follow recipe for Breaded Veal. Lay thick slices of garlic. Spread a layer of canned tomato sauce in skillet, add browned veal and top with ½ cup grated Parmesan cheese. Cover and cook until veal is bubbling hot.

Veal Mozzarella

Follow recipe for Breaded Veal Parmigiana. Lay thick slices of mozzarella cheese, ¼ inch thick, over tomato sauce before topping with browned veal. Cover and cook slowly at 250° until mozzarella cheese is melted. Serve at once.

Veal Milanese

Serve sautéed veal with lemon quarters and sprigs of parsley.

Wiener Schnitzel

Follow recipe for Breaded Veal. Set aside veal. Remove fat from skillet and heat an 8-ounce can of tomato sauce with ¼ cup Medium White Sauce. When very hot, surround veal with sauce and serve garnished with parsley. Lemon slices, slices of hard-cooked eggs, anchovies and beets are suitable accompaniments.

Schnitzel à la Holstein

Follow recipe for Breaded Veal. Just before the veal is browned, open an egg (per serving) in hot fat along edges of pan and fry sunny-side up (or once over lightly). Top each serving of veal with a fried egg and an anchovy. Garnish with lemon wedges.

Saltimbocca (Veal Roman Style)

    16 very thin veal slices (cut from leg)
     8 thin slices prosciutto or cooked ham
     8 slices mozzarella cheese
     1 teaspoon salt
    ½ teaspoon pepper
     3 tablespoons butter
    ½ cup marsala wine

The veal must be cut very thin, then trimmed neatly at home into pieces about 2½ inches square. Cover them with matching pieces of ham and cheese, then top with another slice of veal. Season with salt and pepper. Fasten with toothpicks. Heat butter in skillet set at 300°. Sauté veal sandwiches on both sides until golden, then remove from pan. Quickly add wine to pan, heat quickly without boiling and serve over meat. Serve with a cooked green vegetable. Serves 4 or 5.

Veal Chops with Herbs

> 6 veal chops, ¾" thick
> Flour seasoned with salt and pepper
> 3 tablespoons olive oil
> ½ cup hot water
> 3 tablespoons butter
> 2 tablespoons fresh chopped parsley
> 2 tablespoons fresh chopped chervil
> 2 teaspoons lemon juice

Dust chops with seasoned flour and brown on both sides in oil in skillet heated to 300°. Add water. Cover pan, leaving vent open and reduce temperature to simmer point. Let cook about 30 minutes. Push chops to the sides of the pan, add butter, chopped parsley, chervil, and lemon juice. Heat quickly then serve chops with the pan juices. Boiled new potatoes and a fresh green vegetable are good accompaniments to make a simple but fine main dish. Serves 6.

Veal Stew

Heat 3 tablespoons oil to 300°, soften ¼ cup each of chopped green peppers and onions, 1 diced eggplant, and 3 diced tomatoes. Season to taste with salt and pepper. Let cook for a few minutes, then put in 1½ pounds veal cut into pieces. Add 1 cup hot water or bouillon, cover, close vent and reduce heat to *simmering* temperature; let cook for about 40 minutes. (Liquid should boil gently when light is on). Serves 4.

Veal Casserole

2 pounds tender veal, sliced thin
2 tablespoons flour
1 teaspoon salt
¼ teaspoon pepper
6 tablespoons butter, margarine, or oil
6 tiny white onions, sliced thin
1 cup mushrooms, sliced thin
4 medium potatoes, cut into balls with a melon scoop, or into chunks
2 cups hot chicken stock, or bouillon cubes dissolved in hot water

Pound flour, salt and pepper into veal. Heat pan to 350°. Add butter or oil, sauté veal on both sides until it loses its raw color. Add onions, mushrooms, and potatoes, and brown them lightly. Sprinkle potato balls with paprika, arrange as border around skillet. Reduce heat to simmering temperature. Cover and cook 40 minutes until veal is tender. Add more stock as necessary. Cooking time: 45-55 minutes. Yield: 6 servings.

Lamb Chops in Burgundy

Remove fat from loin lamb chops. Set skillet at 325°, add 2 tablespoons butter and brown chops with small white onions, carrots and 1 cup sliced mushrooms. Add ½ cup Burgundy wine, cover pan, keep vent open, and cook slowly at simmering temperature for half an hour until chops are tender.

Breaded Lamb Cutlets

6 loin lamb chops, cut thin
2 eggs
3 tablespoons water
1 teaspoon salt
¼ teaspoon pepper
Dash of cloves
1 cup fine bread crumbs
3 tablespoons butter, oil, or shortening

1. Remove fat from chops and pound them until very thin. Beat eggs with water, add seasonings. Dip chops into egg mixture, roll in crumbs. Repeat egg-crumb dip.

2. Heat pan to 300°. Melt butter or other fat; brown chops on both sides, turning once. Place on absorbent paper to dry. Two-inch sections of scallions and pieces of tomato (well seasoned) may be sautéed with lamb. Cooking time: 4-7 minutes. Yield: 3 servings.

Pan-Broiled Lamb Chops

Remove fat from chops, and rub them with garlic if you like. Preheat pan, sear chops quickly on both sides at 325°, lower heat to 275° and pan broil them until done. Pour off fat as it accumulates. Allow 10 minutes for a 1-inch chop. For thicker chops, add ½ cup consommé to pan after they are seared, and cook them with cover on and vent open.

Roquefort Chops

Mash Roquefort cheese with a few drops of Worcestershire sauce and spread over the tops of Pan-Broiled Lamb Chops 5 minutes before they are ready. Cover, open vent and serve when cheese is soft.

Patlijian (Lamb, Eggplant and Tomato Stew)

1 pound leg or shoulder of lamb, cut into large dice
3 tablespoons fat
2 small eggplant, cut into large dice
1 medium onion, diced
2 small tomatoes, cut into small pieces
1 teaspoon paprika
Salt and pepper

Preheat skillet to 250°, add fat and lamb. Brown meat lightly. Pour in enough water to make a thin film at the bottom of the skillet. Add onions and when they are soft, add diced eggplant, tomatoes, salt, pepper, paprika and more water to barely cover. Cook for 1 hour at simmering temperature— liquid should boil gently when light is on. Serves 4.

Turkish Lamb Rolls

1 pound raw lamb
1 small onion
1 tablespoon walnut meats
1 tablespoon seedless raisins
1 teaspoon salt
¼ teaspoon cinnamon
2 tablespoons butter
1 egg, slightly beaten
1 cup all-purpose flour
4 tablespoons oil for pan

1. Put lamb, onions, walnuts, and raisins through food chopper, using fine blade. Grind twice. Mix with other ingredients (except shortening). Shape into 8 narrow rolls about 3 inches long.

2. Heat pan to 380°, add oil, brown rolls on all sides, drain on absorbent paper. Allow 2 rolls for each serving. Cooking time: 10-12 minutes. Yield: 4 servings.

Lamb Stew with Dumplings

3 pounds lamb, cut into 2-inch pieces
1 clove garlic
3 tablespoons flour
2 teaspoons dried rosemary (optional)
2 teaspoons salt
½ teaspoon pepper
3 tablespoons cooking oil
2½ cups canned tomatoes
1 cup cooked peas (fresh, canned or frozen)

Dumplings

1 cup sifted all-purpose flour
1½ teaspoons baking powder
⅓ teaspoon salt
½ teaspoon marjoram
½ cup milk

1. Rub lamb with garlic. Shake in paper bag containing flour, rosemary, salt and pepper.

2. Heat pan to 350°. Add oil, brown lamb on all sides. Add tomatoes, and bring to a boil.

3. Reduce heat to simmering temperature. Cover, and cook for 1½-2 hours. Add boiling water as necessary. Turn meat occasionally. About 20 minutes before lamb stew is done, make dumplings: Sift together dry ingredients, add milk.

4. Increase heat to 300°. Drop in dumpling dough with tablespoon, away from sides of pan to avoid scorching. Cover and continue to cook. Just before stew is ready, add peas, and serve as soon as they are hot. Cooking time: 2¼-2½ hours. Yield: 6 servings.

Ham and Potato Skillet

1. In skillet at 325° brown 1-lb. slice ready-to-eat ham in 1 tablespoon butter or margarine and 1 tablespoon brown sugar. Remove ham, pour off drippings.

2. Mix in same skillet 1 can cream of mushroom soup, ⅔ cup evaporated milk (1 small can), ⅓ cup water, ¼ cup cut-up onion, ½ teaspoon salt and ⅛ teaspoon pepper. Stir in 3 cups thinly sliced, peeled raw potatoes and 1 cup sliced raw carrots.

3. Cover, cook over low heat stirring now and then, until vegetables are tender, 35 minutes. Place ham on vegetables. Cover and cook about 10 minutes more. Makes 4 servings.

Ham, Egg, and Banana Grill

    2 tablespons butter or margarine
    ½ pound ham, ¼-inch thick
    2 firm bananas, peeled
    2 eggs

Cut ham into 2 portions. Heat pan to 300°. Melt butter or margarine. Sauté ham and bananas, turning so they brown evenly. Break eggs, and slip, one at a time, into pan. Continue frying until eggs are set. Cooking time: 15-20 minutes. Yield: 2 servings.

Pan-Broiled Bacon

Put bacon into cold skillet, set temperature at 300°, and as soon as slices are warm separate them. Let cook, pouring off fat as it accumulates. Drain on absorbent paper.

Pineapple-Hamburgers

½ pound ground ham, put through food chopper
½ pound ground chicken, put through food chopper
½ teaspoon salt
1 egg, slightly beaten
2 tablespoons fine dry bread crumbs
2 tablespoons oil
4 slices canned pineapple, drained
4 sweet potatoes, pared and halved
¼ teaspoon cinnamon
¼ cup brown sugar
½ cup pineapple sirup

1. Blend together ground ham, chicken, salt, egg and crumbs. Shape into 4 patties.

2. Heat pan to 380°. Add oil, quickly brown patties, turning once. Place pineapple slice on each patty, saving pineapple sirup for later use. Arrange sweet potatoes between patties. Sprinkle with cinnamon and brown sugar. Pour sirup over all.

3. Reduce heat to simmering temperature. Cover pan, close vents, and cook at low simmering point until potatoes are tender. Uncover and spoon pan gravy over fruit and potatoes during the last few minutes to glaze them. Cooking time: 40-45 minutes. Yield: 4 servings.

Sausages

Panbroil sausage links in cold frypan set at 300° until golden brown on all sides. Do not pierce skin when turning. They should be done in 15 minutes or even less, depending on size. (Follow package directions for Brown-and-Serve sausages.) Perfect partners are apple or pineapple rings fried in sausage fat. Also try: Cut cooked sausages into slices, remove fat from pan, pour buckwheat pancake batter over slices, bake at 380°, turning once.

Savory Frankfurter and Cabbage

6 tablespoons bacon fat
2 small onions, minced
4 cups canned sauerkraut
1 medium potato, grated
1 tablespoon caraway seed
Water to cover
8 frankfurters

1. Heat pan to 350°. When pan is hot, add bacon fat and onions. Brown lightly. Toss in sauerkraut, loosen with fork, and let cook about 5 minutes, stirring frequently. Add grated potato and caraway, cover with water, and bring to boil.
2. Cover pan, and cook for 40 minutes. Add frankfurters, whole or cut up, cover again and cook 20 minutes longer. Cooking time: About 1¼ hours. Yield: 6-8 servings.

Frankfurter and Bean Casserole

10 frankfurters cut into 1" pieces
1 green pepper, diced large
½ pound fresh mushrooms
3 tablespoons oil
8 ounce can condensed undiluted tomato soup
1 lb. 4 oz. can baked beans

Brown frankfurters, green pepper and mushrooms in oil in frypan set at 300°, turning them to brown all surfaces evenly. Add tomato soup and baked beans, cover and let cook at simmering temperature until beans are steaming hot. A good Sunday supper dish. Serves 8. Green pepper is a "controversial issue" for some digestions. I dice them rather large so that they can be removed from the plate should anyone wish to do so.

Sweet Cherries and Pork Chops

This recipe was developed by Emma States of Pacific Kitchens. It has an unusual quality but is easy to follow and makes a hearty main course for a winter dinner.

1 No. 303 can dark or light sweet cherries, pitted
¼ cup slivered almonds
6 whole cloves
1 tablespoon vinegar
4 pork chops
3 tablespoons cooking oil
Salt and pepper

Combine cherries and the syrup from can with almonds, cloves and vinegar. Heat oil in skillet set at 350°; when light flashes off, add chops and brown them on both sides. Season with salt and pepper. Pour cherry mixture over chops, lower heat to 250° and simmer covered for thirty minutes or until chops are done. 4 servings. Good winter fare with baked sweet potatoes and broccoli.

Pork Chop Casserole

1½ pounds pork chops
1 teaspoon salt
¼ teaspoon pepper
¼ cup water
4 green peppers, cut into quarters and seeded
4 thick slices of tomatoes

Cut off excess fat from chops. Put them into cold pan. Heat pan to 300°. Brown chops on both sides. Add water, cover pan. Reduce heat to simmer until chops are almost done. Add peppers and tomatoes, cover and simmer 10 minutes longer until they are tender, and serve. Cooking time: About 30 minutes. Yield: 4 servings.

Cantonese Spareribs

    4 pounds lean pork spareribs, cut into 2" pieces
    ¼ cup soy sauce
    1 tablespoon sugar
    ½ teaspoon salt
    Dash of ginger
    1 clove garlic, crushed
    3 tablespoons cooking oil
    2 cups water
    1 cup syrup from canned pineapple
    2 tablespoons cornstarch
    ¼ cup water
    2 cups canned pineapple chunks
    1 green pepper, cut into 1" squares

Combine soy sauce, sugar, salt, ginger and crushed garlic and let stand. Heat oil at 250°, and sauté spareribs on both sides for about 15 minutes. Pour off excess fat. Add pineapple juice and water and simmer, covered and with vents closed, for 1 hour or until tender. Add more water as needed. Turn ribs several times. Push ribs to sides of pan. Combine cornstarch and water and stir into middle of pan. Cook for ten minutes, add pineapple and green pepper and cook 5 minutes longer. Serve with wedges of tomato over cooked rice. Serves 4 or 5.

Sausage and Baked Bean Casserole

Panbroil 1 pound sausages in cold frypan at 300°. Pour off fat. To pan add 1 can (1 lb. 4 oz.) baked beans, 1 can (10-oz.) tomato soup, and 8 whole cloves. Top with sausages, cover, close vents and cook at simmering temperature until very hot. Serves 8 to 10.

Barbecued Spareribs

4 pounds pork spareribs
2 tablespoons fat
¼ cup soy sauce
1 teaspoon sugar
1 clove garlic, peeled
¼ cup sherry wine

Have spareribs cut into serving pieces. Preheat pan to 350°, add fat, brown ribs on both sides. Add other ingredients, and bring to boil. Cover. Reduce heat to simmering. Let steam, covered, about 1½ hours until tender. Cooking time: 1½- 1¾ hours. Yield: 4-6 servings.

CHICKEN IN MANY VERSIONS

32 RECIPES

Recipes in This Chapter

Barbecued Chicken in Foil Packages, 111
Chicken Dinner in the Skillet, 111
Southern-Fried Chicken, 112
Chicken in a Ring, 112
Chicken Hash, 112
Batter-Fried Chicken with Cream Gravy, 113
Pollo Con Arroz, 114
Paella, 115
Carolina Chicken Pilau, 116
Hungarian Chicken with Sour Cream, 116
Braised Chicken with Sherry Wine, 117
Chicken Stew with Dumplings, 118
Dumplings, 118
Chicken Cacciatore, 119
Chicken Fricassee for Four, 119
Chicken Sukiyaki Chafing Dish, 120

Chicken à la King, 120
Chicken in Fruit, 122
Chinese Diced Chicken and Almonds, 123
Breast of Chicken in Wine, 124
Easy Chicken Divan, 124
Stuffed Drumsticks, 125
Chicken and Spaghetti Casserole, 125
Deep-Fried Chicken Pies, 126
Chicken Chow Mein, 127
Chicken Giblets, 127
Perfect Chicken Croquettes, 128
Coq au Vin Chateaubriand, 129
Chicken Curry in Avocado with Pineapple Rice, 130
Chicken and Ham Skewers, 131
Canard au Cinzano Rouge, 131
Duck Mandarin, 132

Barbecued Chicken in Foil Packages

Cut chicken into serving pieces, season, and put in individual wrappings of aluminum foil. Spread generously with barbecue sauce (about 2 tablespoons per package). Close packages so sauce cannot spill out. Bake at 325° for about an hour. Serve in packages, with chunks of French bread to soak in the delicious gravy you will find in the package.

If you have not yet discovered the delight of cooking food wrapped in foil, you have a great surprise coming. Food retains its moisture and does not dry out—the packages are easy to serve at informal meals—and dish and potwashing is reduced to a minimum. Best of all, there is an element of mystery in the wrapped package that appeals alike to youngsters and adult guests. Fish, meats, vegetables can all be cooked this way. Although wrapping foods in paper before cooking is a classic technique—called *en papillote* in culinary language—it is still relatively unused. You will enjoy it. Incidentally, although this sounds like a commercial for aluminum foil unfortunately no one has paid for it.

Chicken Dinner in the Skillet

Husk corn on cob, remove silk and place each ear on a large piece of aluminum foil. Brush with melted butter, salt and pepper (barbecue sauce too if you like). Seal foil with double fold and twist ends to make tight package. Cook with barbecued chicken. Delicious! Shelled fresh peas with thin slivers of mushrooms, 2 tablespoons butter and water, salt and pepper, foil wrapped, will be cooked at the same time. Ideal for small-family cooking.

Southern-Fried Chicken

1 cut-up broiling chicken, 2-3 pounds
¾ cup all-purpose flour
2 teaspoons paprika
2 teaspoons salt
¼ teaspoon pepper
½ cup shortening for pan

1. Wash and dry chicken. Put the flour and seasonings in a paper bag and shake the chicken, a few pieces at a time, in the bag. Add fat to pan.

2. Heat to 360°. As soon as light goes off, indicating that fat is at right temperature, arrange the meatiest pieces in pan, fit smaller pieces around them. Let chicken brown on all sides, turning once. Reduce heat to 260°.

3. Cover pan, vent open, and cook until chicken is fork-tender. Test the drumstick to be sure. To crisp chicken raise temperature to 350° and fry uncovered for the last 5 minutes. Cooking time: 30-40 minutes. Yield: 2-3 servings.

Chicken in a Ring

Prepare pancake batter as on page 168. Remove fried chicken from skillet and keep warm. Quickly wash pan. Make pancakes about 1½ inches in diameter. Serve in an overlapping row around chicken. No bread needed.

Chicken Hash

Soften 1 cup combined minced onion and green pepper in 300° frypan, in 2 tablespoons hot fat. Stir in 3 cups finely chopped cooked chicken and enough condensed cream of chicken soup or white sauce to moisten (about 1½ cups).

Stir in 2 tablespoons minced parsley. More white sauce may be poured over the top. (Condensed cream of mushroom or chicken soup with a few tablespoons cream or milk added make an accepted sauce).

Batter-Fried Chicken with Cream Gravy

Quick Batter: 1 cup pancake mix combined with ½ cup water.

> 1 disjointed broiling chicken, about 2½ pounds
> 1 cup all-purpose flour
> 2 teaspoons baking powder
> 1 teaspoon salt
> ½ teaspoon poultry seasoning
> 1 egg, slightly beaten
> ½ cup milk
> 5 tablespoons fat for pan
> ¼ cup flour (for gravy)
> 2½ cups cream

1. Wash and dry the chicken. Combine the flour, baking powder, salt, poultry seasoning, egg and milk. Dip chicken pieces in this batter, let excess drip off.

2. Preheat pan. Heat fat at 350°. When light goes off, put chicken (meaty pieces first) into hot fat and brown on both sides. Turn without piercing chicken.

3. Cover pan at an angle so steam escapes and continue cooking until chicken is tender (test drumstick with fork). Transfer to platter. Pour off all but 3 tablespoons fat, add flour and stir until smooth. Loosen all the bits that cling to pan. When flour is lightly brown stir in cream. Simmer at 200°, stirring, until gravy is thick. Season just right and serve over chicken. Cooking time: 30-40 minutes. Yield: 3 to 4 servings.

Pollo Con Arroz

A savory Spanish chicken and rice casserole. Can be done ahead and reheated.

1 cut-up roasting chicken, 4-5 pounds
¼ cup olive oil or lard
1 cup raw rice
2 cloves garlic, mashed (optional)
3 tomatoes, chopped
½ onion, chopped
¼ cup carrots, cleaned and sliced
3 threads Spanish saffron
2 whole cloves
2 teaspoons salt
¼ teaspoon pepper
1 cup boiling water or chicken stock
¼ cup sherry wine
2 tablespoons parsley
1 sweet red pepper, seeded and sliced

1. Wash and dry chicken. Heat pan to 300°. Pour in olive oil or lard, add rice and garlic and cook until golden, stirring constantly. Move rice to sides of pan. In center of same pan, adding more oil if necessary, brown chicken on all sides. Add tomatoes, onion, carrots, saffron, cloves, salt and pepper. As soon as they boil, pour in water or stock, and sherry. Add browned rice, bring to boil again.

2. Lower heat to simmering point. Cover pan and cook until chicken is tender. Add small amounts of water if required, but do not let this get too liquid. Garnish with parsley and red pepper. Serve from pan. Cooking time: 1½ hours. Yield: 6-8 servings. (Pan is at correct simmering temperature if liquid boils gently when light is on).

Paella

Garnish the paella with strips of pimento and large cooked shrimp. Surround it with a ring of artichoke hearts into which you can tuck a button mushroom. Cooked lobster is frequently added to the paella at the end.

       1 cut-up frying chicken
       3 tablespoons butter or oil
       1 medium onion, chopped
       1 garlic clove, mashed
       1 bay leaf
       ¼ teaspoon thyme
       2 teaspoons salt
       ¼ teaspoon pepper
       1 pinch of saffron
       1 cup canned tomatoes
       3 cups chicken stock (made from giblets) or bouillon
       1 cup rice
       1 package quick-frozen peas
      24 shrimps, cleaned

1. Clean and dry chicken. Heat pan to 320°. Add butter or oil, brown chicken on all sides. Remove to a platter for later use.

2. Add onion, garlic, bay leaf, thyme, salt, pepper and saffron. Cook for a few minutes, then pour in tomatoes and chicken stock. Bring to boil. Add rice, and as soon as boiling starts again, reduce heat to simmering.

3. Add chicken to pan, simmer until chicken is tender, rice puffy. Turn in peas and shrimp. Let shrimp steam for about 5 minutes or until tender. Serve immediately. If liquid cooks out, add more chicken stock. Cooking time: About 1 hour. Yield: 4 servings.

Carolina Chicken Pilau

    5 cups water
    1 cut-up roasting chicken, 4-5 pounds
    1 teaspoon salt
    ⅛ teaspoon pepper
    1 cup rice
    1 cup seedless raisins
    ¼ cup blanched almonds
    ½ teaspoon curry powder

1. Pour water into pan, cover it, and heat at high temperature. As soon as water boils (8-10 minutes) add chicken, reduce heat to simmering temperature. Cover and cook without boiling until chicken is tender, 45 minutes to 1 hour. Turn it once. Sprinkle with salt and pepper about 10 minutes before it is done. Transfer chicken with slotted spoon to platter, cover and keep warm.
2. Add rice and bring to boil, then reduce heat to simmering. Cover pan and let rice cook gently until it is soft, about 40 minutes. Turn off heat, stir in almonds, raisins, and curry powder. Spoon rice and broth into individual bowls, add pieces of cooked chicken, and serve with hot biscuits. Canned peas may be heated in pan and served with pilau. Cooking time: 1¼ hours. Yield: 6 servings.

Hungarian Chicken with Sour Cream

    1 cut-up broiling chicken, about 3 pounds
    4 tablespoons flour
  1½ teaspoons salt
    2 tablespoons butter or lard
  1½ tablespoons paprika
    ⅛ teaspoon pepper
    1 onion, chopped
    ½ cup water
    ½ cup sour cream

1. Wash and dry chicken. Combine 4 tablespoons flour and salt, in paper bag. Shake chicken in bag, a few pieces at a time.

2. Heat pan to 320°. Add butter or lard, tilting pan so grease spreads all over. Brown chicken on all sides. Add paprika, pepper, onion, and water.

3. Reduce heat to simmering point. Cover pan and cook until chicken is tender. With a slotted spoon transfer to hot platter. Spoon in sour cream, and as soon as it has heated slightly, serve sauce over chicken. *Good Accompaniment:* Cooked noodles with caraway seeds. Cooking time: 50 minutes. Yield: 3-4 servings.

Braised Chicken with Sherry Wine

    1 cut-up broiling chicken, about 3 pounds
    ⅓ cup all-purpose flour
    1½ teaspoons salt
    1 teaspoon pepper
    3 tablespoons oil
    1 cup sherry wine
    2 tablespoons chopped parsley

1. Wash and dry chicken. Combine flour, salt and pepper in bag. Shake chicken in bag, a few pieces at a time, until well coated.

2. Heat pan to 340°, add oil, brown chicken on both sides until golden, about 10 minutes.

3. Reduce heat to simmering temperature. Cover pan and continue cooking slowly for 15 minutes. Pour in wine, cover; cook 15 minutes longer. Combine parsley and pan drippings and serve over chicken. Cooking time: 45 minutes. Yield: 4 servings.

Chicken Stew with Dumplings

1 cut-up fowl, 4-5 pounds
5 cups cold water
1 stalk celery, chopped
4 small white onions
1 tablespoon parsley, chopped
1 bay leaf
2 teaspoons salt
¼ teaspoon pepper
1 white turnip, chopped
2 carrots, chopped

For dumplings

1½ cups sifted all-purpose flour
1½ teaspoons baking powder
½ teaspoon salt
1 tablespoon shortening
2 eggs, slightly beaten
¼ cup milk

1. Clean and salt fowl, see page 36, and put into pan with water, celery, onions, parsley and bay leaf. Heat pan to 300°, bring chicken to boil. This takes about 15 minutes. Remove any scum which rises.

2. Reduce heat to simmering, cover pan and simmer chicken until almost tender, about 1¼ hours. Add salt, pepper, turnip, and carrots and cook 30 minutes longer. Meanwhile prepare dumplings: Sift together flour, baking powder, and salt; cut in shortening. Combine eggs and milk and add to first mixture.

3. Increase heat to 300°, drop dumplings by teaspoon into boiling stew. Cover and cook 15 minutes longer. Serve right from pan. Cooking time: 2 hours; 4 to 6 servings.

Chicken Cacciatore

¼ cup olive oil
1 medium onion, chopped fine
2 green peppers, chopped
1 cut-up roasting chicken, 4-5 pounds
2 bay leaves
1 clove garlic, mashed
½ teaspoon oregano
Salt and pepper
2 cups canned or fresh tomatoes
½ cup canned Italian tomato paste
½ cup chicken stock

1. Add olive oil to pan. Heat to 350°. Sauté onion and peppers lightly, then remove from pan and reserve for later use. Brown chicken on all sides, turning once. Remove from pan. Add other ingredients. Bring to boil, then return browned chicken, onion and peppers to pan.

2. Reduce heat to simmering point. Cover pan and cook until chicken is tender and sauce fairly thick. If sauce is watery, remove cover to thicken it. Do not let all the liquid boil out. Serve with cooked spaghetti, macaroni, or noodles. Cooking time: 1½ hours. Yield: 6-8 servings.

Chicken Fricassee for Four

Heat pan to 340°. In 3 tablespoons fat, brown 3 tablespoons flour, 1 cup chopped onions and pieces of cut-up frying chicken which have been dredged in seasoned flour. Add 3 cups boiling water, 1 teaspoon salt, dash of pepper, small bay leaf, 2 sprigs parsley. Cover. Reduce heat to simmer until tender, 1-1½ hours. Sprinkle with shredded pimentos and black olives.

Chicken Sukiyaki Chafing-Dish

    2 tablespoons salad oil
    1½ cups bamboo shoots, sliced thin
    1 cup raw spinach, shredded
    1 can (8-oz.) sliced mushrooms
    3 chicken breasts, cut into strips
    ¼ cup sugar
    ½ cup water or mushroom liquid
    ½ cup soy sauce
    2 cups sliced green onions, cut into 1" lengths, tops and all

Heat pan to 380°. Pour in oil, tilting so all of pan is greased. Add bamboo shoots, spinach, and mushrooms; sauté lightly on all sides but do not let brown. Push to one side of pan. Add chicken. Combine sugar, water or mushroom liquid, and soy sauce. Pour into pan. When chicken is tender, add green onions; cook 2 minutes more. Stir with wooden spoon and serve right from pan. Cooked rice in individual bowls, assorted pickles, and sliced oranges are excellent Japanese-style accompaniments. Cooking time: 20-25 minutes. Yield: 6-8 servings.

Chicken à la King

    1 disjointed fowl, 4-5 pounds
    4 tablespoons butter
    1 pound mushrooms, sliced thin
    2 green peppers, seeded and chopped
    ½ cup canned shredded pimentos, drained
    6 tablespoons flour
    2 cups chicken stock or consommé
    ½ cup light cream
    1 egg, slightly beaten
    2 tablespoons sherry wine
    Salt and pepper

1. Cook fowl as directed on page 36. Save stock. Remove skin and bones. Cut meat into 1-inch squares.

2. Heat pan to 360°. Melt butter, brown mushrooms, green peppers and pimentos. Transfer to platter to use later. Leave as much butter in pan as possible.

3. Reduce heat to simmering. Stir in flour, slowly add chicken stock and cream. Cook until sauce thickens stirring frequently. Spoon a tablespoon of sauce into egg, then put egg back into sauce. Add chicken and vegetables, stir in wine, season to taste and, when chicken is heated, serve on toast or in toast cases or patty shells. Cooking time: 1¼ hours to boil fowl, then 25 minutes. Yield: 8-10 servings.

Dividend Cooking: At your convenience, prepare dishes that are especially suitable for freezing, then when unexpected guests arrive, or you need a last minute meal—the freezer provides it. Chicken à la king freezes well. Cool thoroughly, pour into pint containers. To serve, heat block in covered pan for about 10 minutes. Remove cover, break into pieces with a fork, cover and cook again at simmering temperature until heated—about 12 minutes. Sauce has a tendency to thicken with freezing—thin by adding chicken stock to frypan.

Note: A four-pound fowl or roasting chicken will yield about 4 cups of cooked, diced chicken.

Chicken in Fruit

>1 cut-up frying chicken, about 3 pounds
>½ cup flour
>2 teaspoons paprika
>2 teaspoons salt
>¼ teaspoon pepper
>½ teaspoon sage
>½ cup fat for pan
>½ cup chicken stock or water
>¾ cup whole cranberry sauce
>¾ cup crushed pineapple
>¼ cup pineapple sirup

1. Wash and dry chicken. Combine in paper bag flour, paprika, salt, pepper and sage. Shake chicken in bag, 2 or 3 pieces at a time.

2. Heat pan to 360°. Add fat, and as soon as it is hot, brown floured chicken, turning as necessary. Allow about 10 minutes. Pour in chicken stock or water, and when it comes to a boil, reduce heat to simmering point.

3. Cover pan and continue cooking for 20 minutes. Combine cranberry sauce, crushed pineapple, and pineapple sirup; spoon over chicken and let cook 20 minutes longer until chicken is dark brown and fork tender. Serve right from pan over cooked rice. Cooking time: 50-60 minutes. Yield: 4 servings.

Simmering temperature—the temperature at which liquid will boil gently when the light goes on.

Chinese Diced Chicken and Almonds

2 pounds breast of chicken
2 tablespoons lard
¾ cup blanched almonds
½ cup chopped celery
3 green onions cut into ½" lengths
1 small piece fresh ginger
1 cup chicken broth or consommé
1 teaspoon salt
¼ teaspoon pepper
¼ teaspoon sugar
2 tablespoons cornstarch
2 tablespoons water
1 tablespoon soy sauce

1. Cut chicken into 1-inch squares and refrigerate until ready to use.

2. Heat pan to 350°. Add lard, brown almonds on both sides. Remove from pan, drain on absorbent paper, and reserve for later use.

3. Add chicken pieces to pan, sauté them lightly on both sides so they lose their raw color, but do not brown. Combine all other ingredients except cornstarch, water and soy sauce and pour into pan.

4. Reduce heat to simmering point. Cover pan and cook chicken until tender, about 20 minutes. Combine cornstarch, water, and soy sauce, add to pan. Continue cooking until sauce thickens, add browned almonds and serve on hot cooked rice. Cooking time: 30-35 minutes. Yield: 4-6 servings.

Breast of Chicken in Wine

Chicken is always a favorite; this one is delicious and easy.

1 pound fresh or frozen chicken breasts, cut in half
2 tablespoons lemon juice
1 teaspoon salt
¼ teaspoon pepper
⅓ cup all-purpose flour
16 small mushrooms
16 small white onions
3 tablespoons oil for pan
1 cup white wine
1 cup chicken stock
Melted butter

1. Brush the chicken breasts in lemon juice, season with salt and pepper, and roll in flour. Brown with onions and mushrooms in pan, heated to 300°, containing cooking oil. Pour in 1 cup white wine, 1 cup chicken stock, cover and cook chicken until soft.

2. Reduce heat to simmering temperature. Cover and continue cooking until tender. Serve immediately with melted butter sprinkled over pieces. (Your electric skillet is so large you can double this recipe and sauté chicken one layer deep.) Cooking time: 20-25 minutes. Yield: 3-4 servings.

Easy Chicken Divan

Prepare cheese sauce in advance. Arrange cooked sliced chicken on cooked buttered broccoli, in large serving platter. Pour sauce over chicken and serve piping hot.

Stuffed Drumsticks

8 chicken drumsticks
3 tablespoons butter
⅓ cup minced cooked ham
⅓ cup finely chopped celery
3 tablespoons cracker crumbs
Salt and pepper
1 egg, slightly beaten
2 tablespoons water
½ cup fine bread crumbs
¼ cup shortening

Pour enough water into skillet to half cover drumsticks, and bring to quick boil; as soon as water boils, add drumsticks, reduce heat to simmering temperature and let cook until tender (allowing about 30 minutes). Turn occasionally. Remove drumsticks and stock (save for sauce). Discard drumstick bones. Melt butter in pan. Brown ham, celery, crumbs. Add salt and pepper to taste. Cool, then use to stuff drumsticks. Combine egg and water, brush on stuffed drumsticks, roll in bread crumbs. Add shortening to pan. Heat pan to 380°. When light goes off, brown drumsticks on all sides (5-8 minutes) and serve crisp. Good with mushroom sauce made with chicken stock. Cooking time: 40 minutes to cook drumsticks; 8 minutes to fry. Yield: 8 drumsticks.

Chicken and Spaghetti Casserole

In skillet set at 350°, melt 3 tablespoons butter, brown ¼ cup each of chopped green pepper and onions, 1 tablespoon each shredded pimentos and parsley. Add 1 cup canned tomatoes, ½ cup chicken stock. Boil for 15 minutes. Add 2 cups cooked spaghetti and 2 cups (more or less) cooked chicken; let warm but do not boil. Serve very hot. Cooking time: 20-25 minutes. Yield: 4 servings.

Deep-Fried Chicken Pies

Flaky and crisp pie crust with a delicious filling.

1½ cups sifted all-purpose flour
½ teaspoon salt
½ cup shortening
¼ cup cold water (about)
½ cup mushrooms, chopped
1 tablespoon butter
1 teaspoon lemon juice
Salt and pepper
Dash of nutmeg
2 tablespoons sherry wine
1 cup cooked chicken, chopped
Shortening for pan ¾" deep

1. Sift together flour and salt, cut in shortening, add just enough cold water to moisten dough. Gather dough into ball, roll about ⅛-inch thick. Now cut into 2½-inch squares.

2. Heat pan to 350°. Make filling: Add mushrooms and butter to hot pan and let brown. Stir in lemon juice, salt, pepper, nutmeg, sherry and chicken and cook for 5 minutes. Turn off heat. Spoon 1 tablespoon chicken mixture into each pastry square, fold into triangles, and seal edges with fork. Add shortening to cleaned pan.

3. Heat pan to 375°. As soon as light goes off, lower pies into hot fat. Increase heat by 10 degrees as cold pies will lower temperature of fat. Fry until pies are brown, turning them once. Drain on absorbent paper. Allow 2-3 pies for each serving. Excellent with tomato sauce. Cooking time: 6-8 minutes. Yield: 10 small pies.

Chicken Chow Mein

3 tablespoons cooking oil
2 large onions, sliced thin
1 cup chicken stock, or bouillon cube dissolved in
  water
1 cup canned sliced mushrooms, drained
1 cup canned bean sprouts, drained
2 cups diced cooked chicken
2 tablespoons cornstarch
2 tablespoons water
2 tablespoons soy sauce

1. Heat pan to 350°. Add oil, and when it is hot, add onions
and a few tablespoons chicken stock. Cover and steam until
soft, but do not scorch. Add chicken stock, mushrooms, and
bean sprouts and bring to boil.

2. Reduce heat to simmering temperature. Add chicken. Mix
cornstarch with water. Stir into pan. Cover, and let simmer
for a few minutes. Add soy sauce, mix well and serve over
fried noodles. Cooking time: 20-25 minutes. Yield: 4 servings.

Chicken Giblets

Cook giblets according to recipe on page 46. Put through
meat grinder, using coarse grind. Sauté in butter with sliced
mushrooms in skillet set at 350°. Add chicken stock to cover,
plus 1 teaspoon lemon juice for each quart of stock. Heat
and serve on toast. Allow 1 set of giblets for two servings.

Perfect Chicken Croquettes

Creamy inside and crunchy outside. Garnish with parsley and spread croquettes with several tablespoons of white sauce. Serve two apiece.

>   3 tablespoons butter or margarine
>   3 tablespoons all-purpose flour
>   1 cup milk or chicken stock (or a combination)
>   1 teaspoon salt
>   ¼ teaspoon pepper
>   2 cups cooked chicken, chopped fine
>   ½ cup cooked ham, chopped fine
>   1 teaspoon lemon juice
>   1 egg, beaten slightly
>   2 tablespoons water
>   1 cup fine bread crumbs
>   Fat for pan ½" deep

1. Heat pan to 200°. Make sauce without waiting for light to go off. Add butter or margarine to pan, and when it melts, stir in flour, milk or chicken stock, salt and pepper. Cook for 5 minutes. Blend in chicken, ham, lemon juice. Refrigerate. When mixture is cool, shape into croquettes or patties, and if possible, put back in refrigerator for several hours (this helps croquettes keep shape). When ready to cook dip croquettes into egg combined with water, then into crumbs; let dry. Add fat.

2. Heat pan to 380°, carefully lower croquettes into hot fat, one layer deep. Fry until brown on both sides, remove with slotted spoon, drain on absorbent paper. Do not let croquettes touch while frying, or they will fall apart. Cooking time: 3-5 minutes. Yield: 8 croquettes.

Coq au Vin Chateaubriand

An elegant chicken cooked with wine, from Alex Hounie of New York's Chateaubriand Restaurant.

> 2 tablespoons butter
> ½ cup diced pork or bacon
> a 3½-lb. chicken (or 2 2-pound chickens) cut into 8 pieces
> 1 teaspoon salt and pepper to taste
> 12 small white peeled onions
> 12 small mushrooms
> 2 tablespoons flour
> 2 minced shallots or small white onions
> 1 minced garlic clove
> 2 cups red burgundy wine

1. Sauté pork or bacon in 2 tablespoons of butter in skillet set at 300°, until brown. Remove and set aside pork scraps. Season chicken with salt and pepper, and brown it in same fat. Add onions and mushrooms, cover and cook over low heat (simmer temperature) until onions are lightly browned, turning occasionally. Allow about 20 minutes so far.

2. Remove everything from the skillet but leave about half the fat. Blend in the flour, minced shallots or onions and the minced garlic. Simmer, stirring constantly until thickened. Turn off heat and gradually add the wine while stirring. Bring back to simmer temperature, add reserved pork and chicken and continue simmering, covered and with vents closed, until chicken is tender, about 1 hour in all. To serve arrange chicken, vegetables and pork in a deep dish, skim off fat from gravy and season to taste. Pour gravy over chicken. (This dish may be prepared the day before serving. It improves by a second heating at low temperature.)

Chicken Curry in Avocado with Pineapple Rice

To simplify the cooking of this dish, you may use a 10-ounce can of condensed undiluted cream of chicken soup thinned out with several tablespoons of cream or milk. Heat and add 4 cups cooked diced chicken. Proceed with step #2.

1. Chop 1 small onion into fine pieces and add to 5 tablespoons butter or rendered chicken fat in skillet set at 250°. Let onion soften, then stir in 5 tablespoons flour, 2 tablespoons curry powder, and slowly add 2 cups chicken stock, 2 teaspoons salt, a dash of white pepper and 1 cup light cream. Cook about 15 to 20 minutes to correct sauce consistency, then add 4 cups cooked diced chicken. Combine by stirring gently.

2. Cut 4 small avocados in half lengthwise. Peel. Squeeze lemon juice over them so they do not lose their color. Arrange them around the electric frypan in an attractive border.

3. Prepare a lazy susan holding chutney, coconut, chopped raisins, chopped onions, and chopped egg yolks, with small service spoons.

4. To serve, put a layer of Pineapple Rice in a circle around individual plates. Set an avocado half in the circle, and spoon hot chicken and sauce over it. Decorate with segments of mango or peeled navel oranges. Guests help themselves to condiments on lazy susan. Serves 8.

PINEAPPLE RICE: Combine and heat 5 cups cooked long grain rice, seasoned with salt and pepper, 2 cups diced canned pineapple, ½ cup toasted almonds or pistachio nuts, and 3 tablespoons butter.

Chicken and Ham Skewers

Cut breast of chicken into thin slices 1½ x ½ inches. Cut cooked ham into matching pieces. Combine 1 tablespoon each of soy sauce, Worcestershire sauce, sherry, and cooking oil, 1 teaspoon sugar, ¼ teaspoon salt, 1 teaspoon cornstarch, and dash of pepper. Spread between chicken and ham. Roll up and thread on skewers. Dip in egg batter (1 egg beaten slightly with 2 tablespoons water). Heat oil in frying pan about ½" deep and when temperature reaches 375° (light goes off) drop in skewers and let cook until golden brown. Serve with skewers arranged attractively on a circle of rice. Sprinkle with chopped scallions; arrange cooked peas outside rice circle. Allow about 4 "sandwiches" for each luncheon serving.

Canard au Cinzano Rouge (Duck in Vermouth)

I found this unusual recipe in a booklet prepared by Harry Botsford for the Long Island Duckling Association. He credits it to Gene Cavallero of the Colony in New York, one of the most famous eating places in the world, and says "The Colony dishes are distinctive enough to make competition bitter about it; they have character and palate-pleasing qualities. This dish is no exception.

"A 4-pound duck is denuded of skin, cut in serving pieces, sautéed in butter until colored golden. Add ¼ cup each of white wine and Cinzano sweet vermouth, flame as the liquid reaches the boil, allow to burn out. Season with a trace of cinnamon; add a minute quantity of tomato paste; cover and simmer until tender. Stir in 1 cup of heavy cream; bring to a boil and serve." About 3 servings.

Duck Mandarin

Rub 2 cleaned ducklings (defrost first if frozen) with garlic.

Cut away large pieces of fat from the cleaned ducklings. Sauté them in their own fat in skillet set at 275°, spooning out excess grease as birds cook. Baste with ½ cup orange and lemon juice. Save drippings and fat. Cool duck, cut off legs and breasts and set aside until ready to use.

Twenty minutes before you are ready to serve, blend 1 heaping tablespoon cornstarch with ½ cup madeira wine and turn into skillet set at 250°. Add 1½ cups orange juice, ½ cup drippings from duck, 1 teaspoon soy sauce and salt and pepper to taste. Cook until sauce is thickened—this will take about 20 minutes. Add the drained sections of 1½ cups Mandarin oranges and heat. Put duck into this sauce in skillet, and serve hot. Keep at 150° or warming temperature if it is to stand.

This dish can be prepared hours or even a day ahead, which makes it ideal for a party. Serve from the skillet over wild rice cooked according to directions on the package.

VEGETABLES THE
SKILLET WAY

44 RECIPES

Recipes in This Chapter

Cooking Vegetables the
   Skillet Way, 135
Asparagus, Ham and Egg
   Casserole, 136
Steamed Broccoli, 137
Brussels Sprouts, 137
Cabbage and Apple Casserole, 138
Cauliflower, 138
Quick Chili Con Carne, 139
Corn on the Cob, 139
Fluffy Corn Fritters, 140
Braised Celery, 140
Stewed Cucumbers, 141
Eggplant Luncheon for Four, 141
French-Fried Eggplant, 142
Kasha and Mushroom
   Casserole, 143
Kasha Varnishkes, 143
Crisp Fried Onions, 143
Batter Fried Onions, 144
Glazed Onions, 144
Peas à la Bonne Femme, 144
Chiles Rellenos, 145
French-Fried Potatoes, 146
Potato Marbles, 146
Shoestring or Julienne
   Potatoes, 146

Potato Curls, 147
French-Fried Potatoes in
   Two Parts, 147
Hashed Brown Potatoes, 147
Souffléed Potatoes, 148
How to Heat Frozen French-
   Fried Potatoes, 148
German Fried Potatoes, 148
Hot Potato Salad for a
   Barbecue, 149
Potato Croquettes, 149
Rice Fritters, 150
Fluffy Rice, 150
Rice Mold, 151
Rice and Raisin Patties, 151
Shrimp Fried Rice, 152
Spinach Patties, 152
Spinach and Noodle Casserole, 153
Sweet Potato and Pineapple
   Puffs, 153
Fried Sweet Potatoes, 153
Lasagne the Quick and
   Easy Way, 154
Tomatoes Provençale, 154
Sautéed Zucchini and
   Tomatoes, 155
Ratatouille, 156

Cooking Vegetables the Skillet Way

Because of its appropriate size, the electric frypan is probably the most practical appliance I have ever used for cooking such large vegetables as asparagus and corn on cob. In addition, however, any vegetable you can name is better when cooked in the frypan because the heat reaches all parts uniformly and quickly, which means good flavor and retention of color and vitamins. General procedures are as follows:

Leafy vegetables such as asparagus, Brussels sprouts (make 2 crosswise slits in the bud ends first), cabbage (shredded to reduce cooking time), cauliflower (separated into flowerets), spinach (only the older leaves, the younger leaves need very little water) should be cooked in actively boiling, salted water until tender when tested with a fork.

Summer squash is delicious when sliced, washed and cooked with ¼ cup water. Be sure you use enough squash to cover the bottom of the frypan, otherwise it will scorch and affect the taste of the vegetable. Cook it long enough to become tender, but still retain its shape; serve with butter. Tomato, eggplant and cucumber need little or no water. They are good stewed in vegetable combinations.

Root vegetables such as carrots, beets, winter squash, potatoes, are best steamed or boiled in only the minimum amount of water necessary to cook them.

Since the maturity of the vegetable is a prime consideration, it is impossible to give exact cooking times. However, when you cook in a frypan which, after all, is far more accessible than an oven or a saucepan placed, let us say, at the back of the stove, it is easy enough to test the vegetable as it cooks. Always, always, always cook it *a point* and not one moment longer.

While we are on the subject of vegetables, I must admit my dissatisfaction with the quality of much of the produce marketed today. Growers seem to care far more about growing varieties for long-distance shipping, rather than for taste. I advise you to select your greengrocer as carefully as you do the butcher, to buy vegetables in season when they are not only cheap and plentiful but also good, and primarily to buy them *young* and small when they are their most tender, rather than large and old. For some reason, many women feel that large vegetables are a great bargain, which they are not. But even young vegetables are no bargain if they are wasted.

Unfortunately, no group of foods can be as unpalatable as improperly cooked vegetables; American garbage pails are filled with proof of this. It seems to me a culinary tragedy that we toss out richly nutritious vegetables and the water in which they cooked, while buying vitamin pills to replace discarded food values. Leftover vegetables are delicious in a hot cream sauce, and the cream sauce itself should utilize the vegetable stock. I hope you will use pages 42 to 51, covering the making of sauces, as an addendum to the section on vegetables.

Asparagus, Ham and Egg Casserole

Break off the tough white part of the 16 asparagus at the bottom of the stalk and rinse the tender part under running water. Cook in skillet set at 350° in actively boiling salted water that covers the asparagus. When tender, drain, cool enough to handle, and roll in 4 medium slices of Virginia ham. Melt 4 tablespoons butter in the pan at 300°, arrange asparagus rolls in a row in the middle of the pan, and sprinkle with a few drops of lemon juice. Open 4 eggs and sauté them at the sides of the pan, turning them once over lightly. Turn the asparagus rolls once also. When ready to serve, sprinkle with salt and fresh pepper, also with grated parmesan cheese if you like. A delightful Sunday brunch to serve right from the skillet with buttered toast points as a border. Garnish with watercress and tomato slices too. Serves 4.

Steamed Broccoli

Remove the tough part of the stalk as well as any bumps on the sides of the broccoli. Cut the stalks into slices about 1″ thick, and quickly rinse the stalks and florets. Put 3 tablespoons olive oil or butter and a clove of garlic (optional) into skillet set at 300°. When oil is hot and garlic is golden, add stalks and florets (the stalks at the bottom so they do not crush the buds). Pour in 6 tablespoons water, salt and pepper. Bring to quick boil at 350°. When water boils, reduce heat to 250°, cover and close vents. Cook about 12 minutes. Do not overcook. The broccoli is at its best when served in this way. One medium sized broccoli serves 4 to 6.

Brussels Sprouts

Make 2 crosswise slits in the bud ends of the sprouts. Drop them into plenty of boiling salted water and cook them at 300° uncovered until tender. A quart of sprouts will serve 6.

Cabbage and Apple Casserole

2 tablespoons butter
4 cups shredded white cabbage
2 large tart apples, pared, cored and sliced
Salt and pepper
1 cup water
¼ cup brown sugar
⅛ cup vinegar

1. Melt butter in pan set at 300°. Add cabbage, apples, salt and pepper. Cook for 5 minutes, stirring constantly.

2. Pour in water. Reduce heat to 220°, cover and cook until cabbage is tender.

3. Add sugar and vinegar, cook for a few minutes longer. Delicious with any kind of pork. Cooking time: about 30 minutes. Yield: 6 servings.

Cauliflower

Separate the flowerets and cook them in actively boiling salted water in skillet set at 300°. Do not cover. For better flavor and to keep it creamy white add a slice of lemon to water when boiling cauliflower. Stir a few tablespoons of White Roux (see recipe) into 2 cups of liquid left from cooking cauliflower to make White Sauce. Grated cheese is a good addition to sauce.

Quick Chili Con Carne

    2 tablespoons fat or oil
    1 clove of garlic, peeled and mashed
    1 onion, finely chopped
    1 pound chopped beef
    2 cups canned red kidney beans
    2 cups canned tomatoes
    2 teaspoons chili powder
    Salt and pepper to taste

1. Heat pan to 300°. Melt fat, add garlic and onion, and cook until tender.

2. Now add beef, and brown thoroughly on all sides. Stir in kidney beans, tomatoes, chili powder, and seasonings. Bring to boil.

3. Reduce heat to 225°. Cover, and simmer for about half an hour. Good winter dish. Cooking time: 45 minutes. Yield: 4-6 servings.

Corn on the Cob

When summer comes, I fall in love with my electric frypan all over again! No barbecue is complete for us unless the frypan is plugged in near the charcoal grill (I had an electrical outlet installed just for this use). Here I cook the vegetables to go with our grilled hamburgers, steaks, chickens and lamb kebabs. We never seem to tire of plain cooked corn on the cob, but I do like to vary the herb butters served with them. Fresh unsalted butter and fresh (finely cut) chives, dill, basil, parsley, sweet marjoram and a drop or two of lemon juice are all creamed together, mixed with salt and fresh pepper and served with cooked vegetables of every kind.

Fluffy Corn Fritters

These are light and delicate, the kind that really do melt in your mouth. If we have any leftover corn, the kernels are scraped off and enough milk or cream added so that they approximate cream-style corn.

> 1 cup sifted all-purpose flour
> 1 teaspoon baking powder
> 1 teaspoon salt
> ¼ teaspoon pepper
> 2 cups cream-style corn
> 2 eggs, slightly beaten
> 1 teaspoon onion juice
> 3 cups fat for pan

Combine flour, baking powder, salt and pepper with the remaining ingredients except shortening, and blend. Put fat into pan. Heat pan to 380°. Grease tablespoon by dipping into hot fat. Spoon up batter and drop into the hot pan. Repeat, dipping spoon into hot fat each time. Fry until golden brown on both sides, turning once. Cooking time: 3-5 minutes. Yield: 30 small fritters.

Braised Celery

Clean celery and cut off root end and tops. Slit lengthwise into 2 pieces. Cover with chicken stock or beef bouillon and cook until tender at 300°. *Do not overcook.* As soon as celery feels soft, take it out of frypan; it gets limp if overdone. Marinate celery in French dressing. Arrange stalks radiating out from center of round plate as if they were spokes in a wheel. Garnish them with crosses made of thin pimento strips. Lay anchovy slices between the crosses. Put cut tomatoes between celery.

Stewed Cucumbers

The cucumbers in our vegetable garden all seem to ripen at the same time. We eat them raw, seasoned with fresh dill and salt and pepper. We eat them in salads topped with sour cream. And finally we cook them and add a new and delicious vegetable to our repertoire.

6 cucumbers, cut into thin slices
¼ cup chopped scallions or onions
3 tablespoons butter
¼ cup vinegar
Salt and pepper

Sauté cucumbers and scallions in butter until very tender (about 20 minutes). Add vinegar, salt and pepper, heat and serve. Serves 4 to 6.

Eggplant Luncheon for Four

1. Peel a large eggplant (or two small ones) and cut into 8 round or long slices about ¼" thick. Sprinkle generously with salt and put between two large plates for at least half an hour. This is essential as it reduces the water content and permits eggplant to fry without absorbing too much fat. Before frying, wash and dry the slices.

2. Dip eggplant slices into milk and seasoned flour. (Best way is to set out two large plates, one with milk, the other with flour.)

3. Heat 1 cup oil in pan at 370° and when oil is hot, fry eggplant on both sides.

4. Pair off eggplant slices, putting a thick slice of American or mozzarella cheese between each pair. Trim off any cheese which extends.

5. Dip the sandwiches into an egg batter (1 egg beaten with 2 tablespoons water), then into corn meal or fine bread crumbs seasoned with ½ teaspoon dried rosemary or marjoram. Set aside for a half hour or so, to let dry.

6. Heat oil to 370° (you will need about ¼ cup). Add eggplant sandwiches and fry them on both sides. Tuck 8 to 10 tomato quarters all around the pan and cook at the same time. Serve together for an unusual lenten luncheon dish; good with cucumbers and sour cream.

French-Fried Eggplant

1 eggplant
¼ cup flour
Salt and pepper
1 egg, slightly beaten
2 tablespoons water
Fine bread crumbs
2 cups fat

1. Cut the eggplant into slices about ½-inch thick. Sprinkle generously with salt and put between two large plates for at least half an hour. This reduces the water content. Drain and dry before using. Cut eggplant slices into fingers or cubes if you wish.

2. Combine flour, salt and pepper. Dip eggplant into seasoned flour, next into egg combined with water, and last, into crumbs. (Best way is to lay out three large dishes, one for each of the dips.) Set aside to dry.

3. Add oil to pan. Heat to 370°. When signal light goes off to show that proper temperature has been reached, drop in eggplant and brown on both sides. Take out pieces as they brown and drain on absorbent paper. Serve quickly as fried eggplant gets soggy if allowed to stand. Cooking time: 2-3 minutes. Yield: 4 servings.

Kasha and Mushroom Casserole

Heat 2 tablespoons rendered chicken fat or other fat in skillet set at 300°. Brown 1 cup sliced mushrooms and ⅓ cup finely chopped onion. Remove from pan and set aside temporarily. Brown 1½ cups buckwheat groats for ten minutes, stirring constantly. This is important, otherwise the kasha will scorch. Add salt and pepper, 3 tablespoons butter or rendered chicken fat and 4 cups chicken stock or consommé. Add browned mushrooms and onions, cover tightly, close vents and cook for 45 minutes, stirring occasionally. Add boiling water if kasha dries. Serves 4-6.

Kasha Varnishkes

Add ½ pound cooked and drained noodle shells and more chicken fat to Kasha and Mushroom Casserole. Heat together and serve.

Crisp Fried Onions

For an even crisper onion, dip in milk before flouring.

    4 large mild onions
    ½ cup flour
    ¼ teaspoon salt
    Dash of pepper
    2 cups fat for pan

1. Cut onions into slices ¼-inch thick. Separate slices into rings. Combine flour, salt and pepper. Dip onions into seasoned flour.

2. Add fat and heat to 370°. When light goes off fry onions until golden brown. Remove and drain on absorbent paper. Cooking time: 4-8 minutes. Yield: 4-6 servings.

Batter Fried Onions

For 4 mild onions, stir together 1 cup of an all-purpose flour, 1 teaspoon baking powder, 1 teaspoon salt, ¼ teaspoon pepper. Beat 1 egg and add to flour. Add ½ cup milk and blend well. Dip onion rings in batter. Fry as above. Drain on absorbent paper.

Glazed Onions

Arrange 2 cups small white onions in pan. Pour over boiling salted water to barely cover. (Or boil water first, add onions.) Bring water to boil again, cover pan and cook at simmering point until they are tender. Drain off water. Move onions to sides of pan. Combine 3 tablespoons brown sugar and 5 tablespoons butter in center of pan. As soon as melted, move the onions around so that they become well coated on all sides. Cooking time: 28-30 minutes. Yield: 4-6 servings.

Peas à la Bonne Femme

        3 tablespoons butter
        4 slices bacon, cut up
       12 green onions, diced
        3 tablespoons flour
          Heart of lettuce, shredded and washed
     1½ cups consommé
        3 pounds peas, shelled
          Bouquet of herbs

1. Melt butter in pan set at 300°. Add bacon and onions and cook until onions are soft but do not let them brown.

2. Stir in flour, add lettuce, pour in consommé, and bring to boil. Let boil a few minutes.

3. Reduce heat to simmering point. Add peas and herbs, and continue cooking 20-30 minutes longer. Remove herbs before serving.

4. To make a herb bouquet, tie 2 sprigs each of parsley and thyme, and ½ a bay leaf, in a piece of cheesecloth about 4 inches square. Cooking time: 25-35 minutes. Yield: 6-8 servings.

Chiles Rellenos

4 bell peppers or whole pimentos, canned
1 pound American cheese cut into chunks 2″ x 1″ x ½″
2 egg yolks, slightly beaten
2 tablespoons flour
1 teaspoon salt
2 egg whites, beaten until stiff
2 cups fat for pan

1. If you are using bell peppers, dip them into boiling water, transfer to paper bag, then close bag to steam peppers for a few minutes. Open and peel skin with a sharp knife. Remove seeds.

2. Cut peeled peppers or pimentos into long strips 2″ wide. Wrap each strip around a chunk of cheese.

3. Make batter: combine egg yolks, flour, and salt. Fold in egg whites. Add fat to pan. Heat to 370°.

4. When proper temperature is reached, spoon peppers into batter, then slide them off the spoon into hot fat. Turn peppers immediately, continue frying, turning once more until brown on both sides. Cooking time: 5-8 minutes. Yield: 4-6 servings.

To make ahead: Follow procedure above. At mealtime, drop the fried peppers into a boiling highly-seasoned tomato sauce. (Heat pan to 380° to boil sauce.)

French-Fried Potatoes

1. Pare 2 large baking potatoes, cut lengthwise into slices ¼-inch thick, then cut each slice into strips ¼-inch wide. If strips are too long, cut in half. Soak in cold water for half an hour. Pour 3 or 4 cups fat into pan, but no more than ⅓ full. (In a 3-quart pan use 1 quart fat.)

2. Heat pan to 380°. Using a long-handled slotted spoon, drop potato chips into hot fat, a few at a time to avoid excessive foaming and cooling of fat. Be sure that pan is never more than ⅓ ful. Fry potatoes until they are as you like them, turning when necessary to brown evenly on all sides. Remove with slotted spoon. Drain on absorbent paper. Season with salt and pepper. Serve hot. Cooking time: 14-16 minutes. Yield: 4 servings. When fat cools, drain and store it for future use.

Note: Fried potatoes get soggy very quickly but they can be kept warm for short periods in oven set at 300°. Keep door open and put them one layer deep on sheets of paper toweling to absorb fat.

Potato Marbles

Pare large potatoes, and cut out balls using a scoop. Follow recipe for French-Fried Potatoes. (Save potato scraps to cook and cream for tomorrow's luncheon.)

Shoestring or Julienne Potatoes

Pare large potatoes, cut into slices no more than ⅛-inch thick, then cut into thin strips ⅛-inch wide. Follow recipe above.

Potato Curls

With vegetable cutter, make raw potatoes into spirals by starting at top and cutting around and downward. Then follow directions for either One or Two Step French-Fried Potatoes.

French-Fried Potatoes in Two Parts

In this recipe, potatoes are partly cooked before they are served, then fried again just before serving.

Part 1. Pare 4 large baking potatoes, cut into slices ¼-inch thick, now into strips ¼-inch wide. Soak in cold water for about 10 minutes, dry between paper towels. Add fat to pan until a scant 1-inch deep. Heat pan to 360°. When light goes off, fry about 1 cup potatoes at a time in hot fat until soft but not brown. Drain on absorbent paper, cover, and put aside until ready to use. Cooking time: 9-12 minutes. Yield: 4 servings.

Part. 2. Cooking time: 6-9 minutes. Add fat to pan as before. Heat pan to 380°. Drop potatoes 1 cup at a time into hot fat, and fry until crisp and brown; turn. Remove with slotted spoon; drain on absorbent paper.

Hashed Brown Potatoes

Combine 3 cups cooked potatoes cut in large dice, with 3 tablespoons flour, 1 tablespoon finely chopped onion, ¼ cup light cream, 1 teaspoon salt and ⅛ teaspoon pepper. Heat 3 tablespoons fat in skillet set at 300°, tipping skillet so that fat covers entire bottom. Add potatoes and press them down with spatula. Serve when good and brown. May also be cut into squares and browned on underside. Allow about 20-25 minutes. Serves 4.

Souffléed Potatoes

These are showy to serve and well worth the effort. The trick lies in using two different temperatures for the fat (easy enough in an electric skillet) and in cutting the potatoes to a uniform size. I always make extras to allow for the ones which do not puff . . . there are always some that won't.

> 2-3 large baking potatoes
> 3 cups fat

1. Pare potatoes, cut into slices ⅛-inch thick. Dry between towels. Add fat to pan. Heat to 300°.

2. Drop potato slices into fat and fry until they are just barely tinged with brown. Remove with slotted spoon. Drain on absorbent paper. Let cool.

3. Heat fat to 400°. Put the cool potatoes into hot fat. In about a minute they should puff. Whether they puff or not, let them cook until they brown. Remove and drain on absorbent paper. Sprinkle with salt and serve. Total cooking time: 14-16 minutes. Yield: 4 servings.

How to Heat Frozen French-Fried Potatoes

Pour a layer of oil into the skillet. Heat to 325°. When light blinks off, add potatoes. Fry until golden brown, turning as necessary. Drain on paper towels and serve hot and crisp.

German Fried Potatoes

Add ¼ cup shortening to pan. Heat pan to 390°. Cut cooked potatoes into large slices. Drop into hot fat and fry until brown.

Hot Potato Salad for a Barbecue

In skillet set at 350°, cook 8 potatoes in boiling water to cover until they are soft. Peel and cut up into large dice. Sprinkle lightly with salt. Set skillet at 250°, melt ½ cup butter, add 3 tablespoons finely chopped green pepper, 3 tablespoons chopped scallions, 1 tablespoon Worcestershire sauce, a dash of celery salt, 2 hard-cooked eggs, diced, and ¼ cup light cream. Add potatoes. Carefully toss together all ingredients, but be careful not to mash potatoes. Keep at lowest or warming heat until ready to serve. Garnish with tiny whole beets and clusters of parsley, serve with barbecued chicken and thick slices of garlicky French bread for an outdoor supper. Serves 6 to 8.

Potato Croquettes

6 medium potatoes, peeled
2 tablespoons butter
1 egg
½ teaspoon grated onion
Salt and pepper to taste
1 egg, beaten slightly
3 tablespoons milk
Fine cracker or bread crumbs
Fat for pan ¾" deep

1. Cook potatoes in boiling water. Drain. Add butter, egg, onion, salt and pepper and mash well. Cool mixture to make shaping easier. Now shape the croquettes as you wish: fingers, balls, cones, or cutlets. Combine egg with milk, dip croquettes into mixture, then into crumbs. Chill in refrigerator until ready to use. (Croquettes hold shape better if chilled before frying.) Add fat to pan. Heat to 370°.

2. Fry croquettes until brown on all sides, turning as necessary. Remove and drain on absorbent paper. Serve with grated Parmesan cheese. Cooking time: 2-5 minutes. Yield: 6-8 servings.

Rice Fritters

    1 cup sifted all-purpose flour
    2 teaspoons baking powder
    ½ cup sugar
    1 teaspoon salt
    ½ teaspoon nutmeg
    2 cups cooked rice
    2 eggs, slightly beaten
    3 cups fat for pan

1. Combine flour, baking powder, sugar, salt, nutmeg, rice and eggs. This is the batter.

2. Heat pan. Add fat. Drop batter a tablespoonful at a time into hot fat and cook until brown. Drain on absorbent paper; sprinkle with powdered sugar or corn sirup. Calas were served with coffee as breakfast bread; the recipe is worth revival. Cooking time: 2-4 minutes. Yield: 18 fritters.

Note: Test batter by dropping a spoonful into hot fat. If it does not hold its shape properly, add a little more flour to remaining batter, and mix well.

Fluffy Rice

Brown rice in a skillet set at 300°. Stir as necessary to brown on both sides. As soon as it is brown, add salted boiling water, in the amount directed on the package, cover pan, vent open, and cook for time specified by brand. Do not stir rice, it will come out fluffy and with separated grains.

Rice Mold

Press seasoned cooked rice into buttered custard cups or other decorative molds, put into skillet, add about an inch of water, cover pan and let steam at 300° until mold is firm. Unmold around creamed turkey or chicken.

Rice and Raisin Patties

These are a good accompaniment for a chicken or ham dish.

> 1½ cups cooked rice
> 1 egg, slightly beaten
> 3 tablespoons chopped seedless raisins
> 1 teaspoon salt
> 1 tablespoon sugar
> 1 egg
> Fine cracker crumbs
> 3 tablespoons butter or margarine

1. Combine rice, egg, raisins, salt, and sugar. Shape into flat patties. Refrigerate if you have time, or use immediately. Dip patties into egg diluted with 2 tablespoons water, and then dip into crumbs.

2. Heat pan to 360°. When light goes off, add butter or margarine, and as soon as it melts, sauté patties on both sides until golden. Sprinkle with sugar. Serve with broiled ham or chicken, or with a sweet sauce for dessert. Cooking time: 5-8 minutes. Yield: 6 patties.

Shrimp Fried Rice

3 tablespoons salad oil
4 cups cooked rice
3 eggs
1 cup fresh cooked or canned cleaned shrimps
1 cup canned bean sprouts, drained
2 tablespoons grated onion
2 tablespoons soy sauce

Heat pan to 340°, add oil, stir in rice, and break eggs into mixture. Scramble. Stir in shrimps, bean sprouts, and onion and cook for 4-5 minutes. Add soy sauce, let cook a minute or two. Serve immediately. Taste for seasoning—if rice was cooked with salt, no more will be needed. Cooking time: 5-7 minutes. Yield: 4-6 servings.

Spinach Patties

2 cups cooked or canned spinach, drained
1 teaspoon parsley
1 tablespoon grated onion
½ teaspoon salt
Dash of pepper
1 tablespoon grated cheese
1 egg
½ cup flour
Fine bread crumbs
¼ cup butter or margarine

Chop spinach and parsley well, and blend with onion, salt, pepper, cheese and egg. Add enough flour to make a stiff paste. Shape into patties and refrigerate for about an hour. Roll patties in crumbs. Heat pan to 370°. Melt butter or margarine, brown patties on both sides, serve hot. Cooking time: 3-5 minutes. Yield: 8 patties.

Spinach and Noodle Casserole

Make 4 cups Cheese Sauce, page 42. Turn into hot sauce in frypan 2 cups cooked well-drained spinach, keeping this more or less to center of pan. Arrange 2 cups fine cooked noodles as border around spinach. Spoon some of the sauce over spinach and noodles. Serve with chicken sandwich, as a good luncheon main course. 6 servings.

Sweet Potato and Pineapple Puffs

    4 medium sweet potatoes, cooked or canned
    2 tablespoons butter
    ½ teaspoon salt
    2 tablespoons crushed pineapple
    ½ cup finely-crushed cornflakes
    2 cups shortening

1. Mash sweet potatoes, add butter, salt, pineapple, and beat lightly with a fork. If mixture is hot, let it cool. When ready to use, shape into balls (dip hands in cold water), roll in cornflakes, chill in refrigerator. Put fat in pan.

2. Heat pan and fat to 370°. Lower puffs into hot fat and fry until brown. Remove and drain on absorbent paper. Cooking time: 2-3 minutes. Yield: 8 puffs.

Fried Sweet Potatoes

Pare 3 large sweet potatoes. Cut into slices or shoestrings. Add fat to pan, ¾" deep. Heat to 375°. Fry potatoes until tender and brown. Cooking time: 8-10 minutes. Yield: 6 servings.

Lasagne the Quick and Easy Way

Put 1 pound of lasagne into the pan—the lasagne size and the pan are perfectly matched—and add as much boiling water as the pan will hold. Set the pan at the very highest temperature, add 3 tablespoons salt and 1 tablespoon oil and cook lasagne until tender (about 10 minutes). Drain well, and remove from pan, keeping noodles flat and unbroken.

The sauce:

> ¼ cup onions, chopped fine
> 3 tablespoons olive oil (or other vegetable oil)
> ¼ pound mushrooms, chopped
> ¼ pound fresh Italian sausage, cut into small pieces
> 3½ cups Italian tomatoes

Sauté onions in oil in skillet set at 300°. Add mushrooms and Italian sausage and cook slowly until fat oozes out from sausage, then add tomatoes. Lower heat to simmering point and cook for 30 minutes or longer if you like. (Italian sausage may be omitted in which case add a mashed clove of garlic to onions before sautéing.) Taste and add salt and pepper if necessary.

Lasagne assembly: Arrange in the following layers in the pan: tomato sauce, lasagne, several thin slices of mozzarella cheese, ricotta cheese, a sprinkling of grated Parmesan cheese. Finish with a layer of sauce. (You will need 1 small mozzarella cheese and 1 pound of ricotta.) Heat for one-half hour in pan at simmering temperature. Serves 6.

Tomatoes Provençale

> 6 firm tomatoes, cut in half
> 4 tablespoons olive oil
> 1 clove garlic, crushed or mashed
> 3 tablespoons parsley (stems removed), chopped
> Salt and pepper

Use medium size tomatoes. Heat oil in pan set at 300°. When hot, sauté the tomatoes with the cut side down. Stick a fork into the top side, and cook for 5 minutes. Turn tomatoes. Combine garlic and parsley and spread over tomatoes, sprinkle with salt and freshly ground pepper and continue cooking, covered, at 250° until soft but do not let them brown and dry out. Serves 4 to 6.

Sautéed Zucchini and Tomatoes

Do you never find enough vegetable casseroles? Here's a favorite.

> 2 pounds zucchini
> 3 tomatoes
> 3 tablespoons butter
> 1 medium onion finely chopped
> 1 clove garlic, mashed
> 1 teaspoon salt
> ⅛ teaspoon pepper
> Sugar

1. Scrub zucchini, cut off ends, and cut into ½-inch crosswise slices. Cut tomatoes into quarters.

2. Heat pan to 400°. Melt butter, add onion and garlic, and let brown lightly. Add zucchini and tomatoes, and sauté on both sides.

3. Reduce heat to simmering. Cover pan and continue cooking until tender, 10-15 minutes longer. Season to taste with salt, pepper, sugar. Cooking time: 16-18 minutes. Yield: 4-6 servings.

Ratatouille

Slice 3 eggplant, sprinkle with salt and put between two plates for at least half an hour to reduce water content. Sauté the slices in 2 cups hot oil (heated to 370°). Drain them on absorbent paper. Remove most of oil. Sauté 1 large minced onion in frypan set at 300°, when onion is golden, add 3 sliced tomatoes and 2 small sliced zucchini. Add 10 Greek olives, 2 mashed cloves of garlic, a dash of rosemary and marjoram, and salt and pepper. Cook for half an hour until eggplant is very soft . . . almost mushy. Serves 6.

EGG AND CHEESE DISHES IN VARIETY

12 RECIPES

Recipes in This Chapter

Perfect Eggs Poached in Quantity, 159
Fried or Sunnyside Eggs, 159
Scrambled Eggs, 160
Baked or Shirred Eggs, 160
Creamed Eggs, 160
Eggs in a Nest, 161

Egg and Zucchini Sauté, 161
Eggs Foo Yoong, 162
Sauce for Egg Foo Yoong, 162
Ham-Filled Omelet Roll, 163
Ring Tum Tiddy for Sunday Supper, 163
Welsh Rarebit, 164

Perfect Eggs Poached in Quantity

Sometimes I wonder how Sunday breakfast was ever cooked in my kitchen! Five eggs poached and ready at one time just were not possible before we acquired a large electric skillet. It had never occured to me to use the large range frypan because the heat was uneven, as much of the pan extended beyond the burner. Anyway here is how I do it now: I put in enough water to come at least half way up the skillet, add 1 teaspoon salt, bring to a boiling point at highest heat (boiling is faster with cover on), open the eggs one at a time into cup, then slip into boiling water. I turn temperature down to 200°, and set timer for 3 minutes (which is the way we like them . . . you may feel differently about this). As the eggs poach, dip some hot water over them to cook the tops. I remove with a slotted spoon in the order in which they were poached, otherwise some will be better done than others when the timer rings.

Fried or Sunnyside Eggs

Melt about 4 tablespoons of butter (which has the best flavor of any of the fats for this purpose) in a skillet set at 275°. When it is hot, and the light goes off, break the eggs into a cup, then slide them into a pan. Put the cover on and the tops will cook without any need for basting. (Whites can also be cut with a spoon so that liquid from top runs down.) Serve when the white is firm but the yolk is still soft, as very few people like the yolks hard. For eggs "once over lightly" turn fried eggs with a pancake turner and remove almost as soon as the heat of the pan touches them . . . do not overcook. Four or 5 eggs can be fried at one time, or white bread can be toasted alongside one or two eggs and served at the same time.

Scrambled Eggs

I like scrambled eggs slightly moist but still quite firm, which is easier to do than to describe. Melt 2 tablespoons butter in a skillet heated to 275°. Beat eggs (allow an average of 1½ for each serving), add salt and pepper, break into skillet, and scramble gently when eggs begin to set. Eggs are delicious with many different foods. Add them to the following which should first be sautéed in the skillet:

> Chopped onions and tomatoes
> Minced bacon
> Chicken livers
> Canned kippers
> Smoked salmon and chopped onions
> Sausages
> Mushrooms

Baked or Shirred Eggs

Break an egg into a buttered custard cup containing a tablespoon of light cream. Sprinkle with salt and pepper, dot with butter and paprika. Cook in frypan containing ¾" water, temperature set at 275°. The cover should be on and the vent open.

Creamed Eggs

Make 2 cups Medium Cream Sauce or Cheese Sauce, page 42 or 43, add 6 hot shelled hard-cooked eggs. Serve hot on toast or in patty shells.

Eggs in a Nest

Melt 3 tablespoons butter in an electric frypan set at 300°. Sauté thin slices of white bread on one side. Turn and cover with a piece of American or Swiss cheese the same size as the bread. Open an egg over each slice, making certain not to break the yolk. Sprinkle with 1 tablespoon of finely chopped green herbs (chives, parsley or marjoram, for instance) or with ½ teaspoon dried herbs which has been softened in hot water. Cut thick slices of firm tomato 1" thick. Sprinkle them with a few drops of onion juice. Dip in cornmeal seasoned with salt and pepper. Arrange tomatoes around the sides of the pan. Cover pan, close vent, set temperature at 250° and cook until eggs are nicely set. Turn the tomato slices once. Sausages may be fried in advance (keep them slightly underdone) then tucked around the rim of the pan to keep warm while eggs and tomatoes are cooked. Serve with creamed cooked spinach for luncheon.

Egg and Zucchini Sauté

 ⅓ cup corn oil
 2 cups thinly sliced small zucchini (2 medium)
 4 eggs
 ¾ teaspoon salt
 ⅛ teaspoon pepper
 4 tablespoons grated Parmesan cheese

Heat corn oil in an electric frypan at 300° F. Add the zucchini and cook, stirring occasionally, until light brown and tender, about 5 minutes. Beat eggs, add salt, pepper and cheese. Blend well. Pour egg mixture over zucchini and cook over medium heat, lifting the edges as they cook. When bottom is browned and while the center is still slightly soft, cut in wedges in pan and turn each wedge to brown other side slightly. Serves 3-4.

Eggs Foo Yoong

    2 tablespoons thinly sliced celery
    ¼ cup French green beans, bean sprouts, or peas in pod
    ¼ cup sliced mushrooms
    1 tablespoon thinly sliced scallion
    2 tablespoons thinly sliced water chestnuts
    ¼ cup cooked sliced or diced chicken, shrimp, or pork
    4 eggs
    ¼ teaspoon salt
    ¼ cup corn oil

1. Prepare vegetables and meat, cutting into thin slices or matchstick pieces.

2. Add salt to eggs, beat until fluffy with beater then stir in the vegetable-meat mixture.

3. Heat 1 tablespoon corn oil in an electric skillet-frypan at 300°. Measure out about ¼ to ⅓ cup of the egg mixture for an individual omelet and pour into heated oil. Several omelets may be made at one time. Cook until bottom surface is delicately brown; turn to cook on other side.

4. Remove omelets, drain lightly on absorbent paper; place on serving dish. These traditional Chinese omelets may be stacked for serving. Makes 4 to 6 small omelets.

Sauce for Egg Foo Yoong

    2 tablespoons cornstarch
    1 cup water
    1½ teaspoons soy sauce
    2 bouillon cubes

Add water gradually to cornstarch in small saucepan and stir until well mixed. Add soy sauce and bouillon cubes. Cook over low heat, stirring constantly, until bouillon cubes are dissolved and sauce is thickened and clear.

Ham-Filled Omelet Roll

5 eggs, beaten
¼ cup milk
Salt and pepper

Heat 2 tablespoons butter in a frypan set at 275°. When hot, pour in eggs and cook about 3 minutes until omelet is brown. Do not scramble eggs, but lift from time to time so that un-cooked portion goes to the bottom. Lift from several differ-ent parts so that the omelet cooks evenly. Spread a cup of diced cooked ham through the center of the omelet, then carefully fold the two sides over the middle. Serve with hot cheese sauce. Makes 4 luncheon servings.

Ring Tum Tiddy for Sunday Supper

¼ cup butter
1 pound sharp Cheddar cheese, cut up
1 cup sweet onions, diced
1 10-ounce can condensed cream of tomato soup
   (undiluted)
1 egg, slightly beaten
1 tablespoon Worcestershire sauce
Dash of Tabasco sauce
½ cup sliced olives

Melt butter in skillet at 275°, sauté onions until soft. Reduce heat to 160°-180°, add cheese and cook slowly until melted, then add soup. Combine egg and seasonings in a cup, add a spoonful of hot mixture to egg, then pour back into skillet. (Egg may curdle if mixed right into skillet.) Simmer until smooth, add olives, stir and serve on plain buttered toast or on toast which has been spread with anchovy paste. Beer is the classic accompaniment. 4 servings.

Welsh Rarebit

Spread 6 half slices of white bread (from which crusts have
been removed) with butter on one side only. Brown them
along the sides of the pan in skillet heated to 300°. Turn
once. Just before second side is done, reduce skillet heat to
160°. Combine ¾ cup cheese, 3 tablespoons pale ale or wine,
a little English mustard, a dash of cayenne pepper, and perhaps a well mashed clove of garlic in the center of the pan.
Let cheese melt, then serve over the buttered toast, sprinkled
with cayenne pepper if desired. Toast may also be made
separately and brought to table when Welsh rarebit is ready.
Serves 3.

THE PANCAKE
AND SANDWICH BAR

29 RECIPES

Recipes in This Chapter

Pancakes

Basic Pancakes, 168
Apple Pancakes, 168
Banana Pancakes, 168
Blueberry Pancakes, 168
Buckwheat Pancakes, 169
Buttermilk Pancakes, 169
Cheese Pancakes, 169
Hawaiian Pancakes, 169
Strawberry Pancakes, 169
Tahiti Cakes, 169
Flaming Crépes Suzette, 170
Potato Pancakes, 171
Easy Pancakes for Filling, 171
Filled Pancakes, 172
Tuna Fish and Cottage Cheese
    Pancakes, 171
French Toast in Kirsch Sirup, 173

Sandwiches

Barbecued Beefburgers, 174
Hot Chicken and Gravy
    Sandwiches, 174
Sandwich Steaks, 174
French Toast Sandwiches, 174
Club Specials, 175
Croque Monsieur, 175
Western Sandwich, 175
Creamed Turkey on Toast, 176
Open Cheese and Tomato, 176
Hot Roast Beef Sandwich, 176
Easy Cheese Blintzes, 177
Bacon, Tomato and Peanut
    Butter Buns, 177
Grilled American Cheese
    Sandwich, 178

Pancakes Pancakes and More Pancakes

Near my home is a busy "snackery" called Pancake House. Summer or winter, the S.R.O. sign is out late in the evening. If you think about the popularity of this unpretentious little place you realize of course that short-order food is perfect for midnight supping, because people simply do not like rich meals late at night. So for your next party, wouldn't it be practical to feature the inexpensive and simple food suggested in this chapter?

Although pancakes do have to be baked at the very last minute, I have managed them successfuly for a small group. Using two skillets—I am sure you will find a neighbor or friend who can spare hers for the evening—it is possible with the help of one person to make enough pancakes at the table or buffet to feed six people. For a bridge-foursome, you can get a head start if dummy plays the last hand for you. (It is only fair to note that the most interesting hand of the evening usually comes when I am plotting to get the food started—if this happens to you, just force yourself to go.)

Another popular feature of Pancake House is the rolling wagon carrying an assortment of sirups. Among them are boysenberry, black raspberry, honey, blueberry, butter pecan, and of course maple. These can easily be made ahead and set up on a tea cart or a lazy susan, adding a little extra touch to a simple little meal.

Basic Pancakes

    1¼ cups all-purpose flour
      1 level tablespoon baking powder
    ½ teaspoon salt
    1½ tablespoons sugar
      1 egg, beaten lightly
      1 cup milk
      2 tablespoons melted shortening

1. Combine flour, baking powder, salt and sugar. Beat egg until it is light, stir in milk and shortening. Quickly pour into dry ingredients and mix together.

2. Heat pan to 380°. Drop pancake batter, about 2 tablespoons at a time, into hot greased pan. Bake until bubbles form over the top, turn and bake second side. Serves 4-6.

Apple Pancakes

Add 1 cup diced raw apple to batter in Basic Pancakes. Bake as directed. Sprinkle with confectioners sugar and serve with sour cream. Or serve in a row around pork chops or barbecued spareribs.

Banana Pancakes

Add mashed ripe banana to Buttermilk Pancake batter.

Blueberry Pancakes

When blueberries are in season, add ¼ cup to batter, make as above.

Buckwheat Pancakes

Follow the directions which come with the package of buckwheat pancake mix. Through the years I have tried many different recipes and the best are always on the buckwheat box.

Buttermilk Pancakes

Substitute buttermilk plus ½ teaspoon soda for the milk called for in Basic Pancakes. Bake as directed.

Cheese Pancakes

Fold ½ cup grated American cheese into Basic Pancake batter.

Hawaiian Pancakes

Tiny chunks of canned pineapple are added to Basic Pancake Batter.

Strawberry Pancakes

Make French Pancakes, roll crushed sweetened strawberries in them, top with ice cream and one large whole berry for each serving.

Tahiti Cakes

Blend shredded coconut into the Basic Pancake Batter.

Flaming Crêpes Suzette

Delicate pancakes . . . delicious sauce . . . made and blazed in the skillet

Part 1.

>   1 cup all-purpose flour
>   2 teaspoons sugar
>   ¼ teaspoon salt
>   3 eggs, slightly beaten
>   1 cup milk
>   Butter for pan

Combine the flour, sugar and salt. Add eggs and slowly stir in milk. Heat pan to 380°. Grease pan lightly with butter. Spoon in about 2 tablespoons batter to make paper-thin cakes about 4 or 5 inches in diameter. Brown on both sides. Spread out on warm platter, or on towels, but do not stack. (You may do this part several hours ahead, roll up pancakes in a towel in one layer and refrigerate until ready to use.)

Part 2.

>   ½ cup butter
>   ¼ cup sugar
>   ½ cup orange juice
>   1 teaspoon grated lemon rind
>   ¼ cup Cointreau
>   ⅓ cup brandy

Heat pan to 360°. Melt butter, add sugar, stir and cook for several minutes. Pour in orange juice and lemon rind, cook until sirup is reduced a half. Turn in Cointreau. Reduce heat to 200°. Transfer pancakes to sauce and as soon as they are moist, flip each one over, first in half, then in quarters. Pour in brandy, let heat (cold brandy won't blaze) then light with match. Spoon blazing sauce over pancakes and serve flaming. Enough for 6-8 servings.

Potato Pancakes

3 medium potatoes, pared
1 egg
4 tablespoons coarse bread crumbs
2 teaspoons grated onion
Salt and pepper
¼ cup oil

1. Grate potatoes just before using or they turn dark. Drain off excess liquid. Add egg, crumbs, onion, salt and pepper, and stir well. If necessary, add more crumbs, but keep batter thin enough to make crisp "cakes."

2. Heat pan to 380°. Add oil, and as soon as light flicks off, drop batter from a spoon into hot oil. Turn cakes to brown on both sides, serve very hot and crisp. Add more oil as needed. The large surface of your automatic skillet bakes many pancakes at one time . . . while you are comfortably seated. Four to six servings.

Easy Pancakes for Filling

Anyone who has made a quantity of crêpes for filling knows how tiresome it is to do them one by one. It seemed to me that in the electric skillet, with its even, over-all heat, it should be possible to do several at one time. After many tests, the following batter and a somewhat lowered temperature seem to work best:

2 eggs, lightly beaten
1 cup water
½ cup flour
½ teaspoon salt
3 tablespoons melted butter
Butter for frypan

Combine ingredients in the order given, then set batter aside for an hour or so to mellow. Spread skillet lightly with more butter. Turn heat to 340°. When butter is hot, pour in about ¼ cup batter (use a ¼-cup measure) tilt the pan quickly to spread batter all over. Brown on one side. Cut the large pancake into 4 or 6 sections and fill them on the browned side as directed in the recipe. (Because of the speed with which the pancakes set, it is possible that some sections will tear; patch them with more batter if you can, if not discard that particular section and use the others.)

Filled Pancakes

Use any leftover cooked food—vegetable, chicken, fish, beef, or seafood—dice well, moisten with cream sauce, and use as filling. Roll up. Sauté filled pancakes in butter at 350°, turning to brown all sides. Serve as hors d'oeuvre or as luncheon dish. For luncheon, top browned filled pancakes with hot Cheese Sauce, page 42.

Tuna Fish and Cottage Cheese Pancakes

    1 cup cottage cheese
    1 small can tuna
    2 tablespoons grated onion
    1 tablespoon finely chopped parsley
    2 eggs, separated
 1½ tablespoons flour
    1 teaspoon baking powder
    ½ teaspoon salt

Blend cheese, fish, onion, parsley, egg yolks, flour, baking powder and salt. Fold in stiffly beaten egg whites. Drop by tablespoons onto greased skillet set at 360°. Brown on both sides. Serve as a nourishing luncheon.

To freshen stale rolls: Sprinkle them lightly with water, wrap loosely in aluminum foil and heat in covered pan (vents open) for ten minutes at highest temperature.

To heat bakery rolls: Wrap in aluminum foil or in a paper bag and heat at highest temperature.

Buttered Bread: Cut slices of white bread in half crosswise, and arrange on aluminum foil with cut sides up. Spread tops and sides with lots of butter. Cover pan and heat for 15 minutes at 375°.

French Toast in Kirsch Sirup

An elegant Christmas breakfast, with fruit en brochette and piping hot coffee.

    2 eggs, slightly beaten
    ½ cup cream or milk
    ¼ teaspoon salt
    1 tablespoon sugar (optional)
    6 slices day-old white bread
    3 tablespoons butter or margarine

Sirup

    6 tablespoons honey
    2 tablespoons butter
    3 tablespoons Kirsch

1. Combine eggs, cream or milk, salt and sugar, beating lightly to mix well. Dip bread slices into egg mixture, coating both sides.

2. Heat pan to 360°. Melt butter or margarine, transfer dipped bread into hot fat, and pan-fry them until brown, turning once. (You can make at least 4 slices of bread at one time.) Remove toast from frypan. With a sponge, pick up browned bits of batter from pan. Add honey and butter and as soon as they are heated, stir in Kirsch. Pour over French toast—serve at once. (You may serve maple sirup, strawberry jam, or cinnamon-sugar mixture in place of Kirsch sirup.) Cooking time: 2-3 minutes for toast, another minute or two for sirup. Yield: 6 slices.

Barbecued Beefburgers

In frypan set at 300° brown 1½ cups chopped meat in 2 tablespoons oil. Add 1 8-ounce can of tomato sauce, 2 tablespoons chili sauce, 2 tablespoons vinegar, 1 tablespoon Worcestershire sauce, 3 tablespoons water, 1 tablespoon finely chopped or grated onion, 1 tablespoon brown sugar, and 1 teaspoon prepared mustard. Reduce to simmering temperature and let cook for 15 minutes. Serve on toasted hamburger buns.

Hot Chicken and Gravy Sandwiches

Make a gravy of 2 tablespoons chicken fat, 2 tablespoons flour, 1 cup chicken broth, salt and pepper, and a dash of Worcestershire sauce. Serve hot over slices of chicken on white bread.

Sandwich Steaks

Cook minute steaks quickly in a little butter or olive oil in pan heated to 420°. Turn them only once. Serve between hot buns. (Buns may be toasted, cut side down, alongside steaks).

French Toast Sandwiches

Any kind of sandwich, provided the filling is not too runny, is good dipped in beaten egg-and-water batter, then sautéed in skillet in butter heated to 360°.

Club Specials

1. Make three-decker sandwiches of thinly-sliced, buttered and trimmed white bread. Use thin slice of turkey for lower deck, thin slice of sharp cheese for upper deck. Make 1 cup batter for each 4 sandwiches, using pancake mix, or follow recipe on page 113. Cut each sandwich into tiny squares or thin strips, and dip in batter.

2. Heat pan to 375°, add ¼ cup butter or margarine and, as soon as it is melted, sauté sandwiches, turning as necessary.

Croque Monsieur

These hot ham and cheese sandwiches are good short-order cooking for midnight suppers. This quantity will serve 6-8.

    1 cup soft butter
    16 slices white bread
    16 thin slices of Swiss cheese
    8 slices ham (same size as a slice of white bread)

Let the butter soften at room temperature. Trim the crusts from slices of white bread, then butter one side using about half the butter. Make sandwiches of cheese, ham, and another slice of cheese. Trim off any bits of food that stick out from the bread. Melt remaining butter in skillet at 275° and sauté sandwiches on both sides. Serve very hot—cheese gets stringy when it cools. 8 sandwiches.

Western Sandwich

Heat 2 tablespoons fat in skillet at 300°. Sauté 2 tablespoons diced onion, 2 tablespoons chopped green pepper, and ½ cup diced ham; add a dash of A-1 sauce and salt and pepper. When onion and green pepper are soft, stir in 3 scrambled eggs. Serve between toast slices. Will make 3 sandwiches.

Creamed Turkey on Toast

Cut in half 6 slices day-old white bread (crusts removed) dip in a batter of beaten egg and 2 tablespoons water. Sauté in skillet at 300°, turning once. Remove to large platter. Heat 2 cups cream sauce and a dash of paprika in skillet at 250°, add 12 small slices of cooked turkey, and heat until turkey is warm; *do not boil it*. Put French toast around the platter alternating with pineapple rings. Spoon creamed turkey into middle. Garnish both sides with clumps of parsley. Serves 6.

Open Cheese and Tomato

Cut firm tomatoes into 4 thick slices, dip in cornmeal which has been seasoned with salt and pepper. Melt 3 tablespoons butter in pan set at 250°, and when butter is melted sauté tomatoes at sides of the pan, for 5 minutes. Turn tomatoes.

Reduce heat to 150°, grate ¼ pound Swiss cheese into the middle of the pan. Stir in 3 tablespoons wine, ½ teaspoon prepared mustard, and a dash of Tabasco sauce.

Combine 2 egg yolks and a tablespoon of milk. Stir some of the melted cheese into the egg, then put it back into the pan. Cook until thick. Serve tomatoes on buttered toast which has been spread with anchovy paste. Top with Swiss cheese sauce. Serve with pickles, olives, and of course beer. A good Sunday supper dish. It should be made at the table since cheese sauces do not stand well. Serves 4.

Hot Roast Beef Sandwich

If possible use the natural juices left from the roast in making the sandwich. If not, make a brown gravy as follows: Heat ¼ cup fat and drippings from roast in frypan, stir in ¼ cup flour very slowly. Stir in 2 cups juices from pan (from which fat has been removed) or water and beef juices combined to make 2 cups. Heat at simmering temperature until gravy is thick and smooth. A dash of Kitchen Bouquet adds flavor.

Place a slice of unbuttered white bread on a plate, cover it with roast beef. Spoon over it some very hot brown gravy or natural pan juices, also heated. Garnish with dill pickle. Serve with a mound of mashed potatoes.

Easy Cheese Blintzes

1. Combine 1 pound cottage cheese, salt, and a pinch of pepper. Mash well with a fork. Stir in 2 lightly beaten eggs and mix again.

2. Cut away the crust from a loaf of thinly sliced white bread (about 1 pound). Roll each slice very thin with a rolling pin. Sprinkle with a mixture of cinnamon and sugar.

3. Place a tablespoon of the cottage cheese mixture in the middle of each slice of bread, and pinch ends together to seal. Wrap in wax paper until ready to use.

4. Fry in a generous amount of melted butter (about 6 tablespoons) in skillet set at 325°. Turn once. Serve hot with sour cream and slightly crushed sweetened strawberries. Will make about 20 "blintzes".

Bacon, Tomato and Peanut Butter Buns

For each sandwich, spread a hamburger bun with peanut butter. Fry 3 slices of bacon in cold frypan set at 340°. When brown and crisp on both sides, dry on absorbent paper. Pour off most of fat from pan. In fat which clings to pan, sauté a thick slice of seasoned tomato on both sides. Put tomato on bun with 3 slices of bacon. Mayonnaise may be served separately.

Grilled American Cheese Sandwich

Always popular for a quick luncheon. Make a sandwich of two slices of white bread and a slice of American cheese trimmed to fit. If you wish, spread the cheese with pickle relish, ketchup, deviled ham or tongue, etc. Spread soft butter on the outside of both slices of bread and brown in frypan preheated to 360°. Takes a few minutes.

FRUITS, DESSERTS, SWEETS AND BEVERAGES

20 RECIPES

Recipes in This Chapter

Applesauce, 181
Apples with Fruit Filling, 181
Pommes Sauté, 181
Pears in Wine, 182
Hot Fruit Sauce, 182
Brandied Peaches, 182
Tea Cakes, 183
Southern Berry Pies, 183
Christmas Cookies, 184
Skillet Peach Brown Betty, 185
Easy Apple Fritters, 185

Fruit Flambé, 186
Blazing Cherries Jubilee, 186
Stewed Oranges, 186
Fruit Fritters, 187
Poaching Fruit, 187
Kumquat Garnish for
  Pineapple, 188
Large Pineapple Upside-Down
  Cake, 188
Hot Coffee-Chocolate, 189
Café Brulot, 190

Applesauce

    2 pounds tart apples
    ¾ cup water
    ½ cup sugar
    Dash of lemon juice

Cut apples into quarters. Do not peel. Remove cores. Put apples into pan, cover with water. Heat pan to 250°. Simmer until apples are tender. Strain, add sugar and lemon juice and stir until sugar dissolves. Serve warm or chilled. Cooking time: 20-25 minutes. Yield: 6 servings.

Apples with Fruit Filling

Core 6 apples. Pare off 1-inch of peel around the stem. Arrange apples in pan, stem side up. Fill centers with drained crushed pineapple or puréed cooked apricots. Combine 1 cup sugar and ½ cup water. Pour over apples. Dot each apple with butter.

Heat pan to 320°. As soon as sirup boils, cover pan, close vent, reduce heat to simmering. Cook, basting several times, until apples are tender. Remove cover. Add 3 drops each red and yellow food colorings to sirup in pan. Mix well to blend colors. As sirup boils, spoon it over the apples. Serve hot from pan with cream or refrigerate and serve cold. Baking time: 25-35 minutes. Yield: 6 servings.

Pommes Sauté

Melt 3 tablespoons butter in skillet set at 275°, add ½-inch-thick rings of red unpared apples from which center has been removed. Sauté until soft, about 6-8 minutes. Serve as meat garnish.

Pears in Wine

Boil sirup from a large can of pears until reduced in half, then lower temperature to simmering and warm pears. Make whipped cream laced with a dash of rum or cognac. Serve pears and sauce in dessert plates, cover with whipped cream and pass toasted crushed almonds in a small dish to sprinkle over the cream.

Hot Fruit Sauce

> 1 cup sugar
> 1 tablespoon flour
> 1 cup pineapple sirup (or any other canned fruit sirup)
> 1 egg yolk
> Dash of lemon juice

Combine sugar and flour and stir into sirup. Simmer in pan at simmering temperature, for ten minutes. Add a tablespoon of hot sauce to the egg yolk and return to pan with a dash of lemon juice. Serve hot over fruit cups. Or make crêpes (page 170), fold them first into halves then into quarters, cover with a damp towel and refrigerate until ready to use. At serving time put folded pancakes into hot sauce just long enough to warm them. Makes enough sauce for 4 servings, 3 pancakes to a serving.

Brandied Peaches

Pour some of your good brandy into the skillet and warm at low temperature (alcohol boils away quickly so just barely heat it) turn temperature off, light a match to brandy at one edge and serve over cooked (canned) peaches, with or without vanilla ice cream.

Tea Cakes

Delicious, featherlight and delectable

6 tablespoons sugar
2 eggs, well beaten
½ cup sifted all-purpose flour
½ teaspoon nutmeg
Oil for pan ¾" deep

Combine sugar and eggs. Beat well. Sift flour and spice and add to the mixture. Add more flour if necessary. Put oil in pan.

Heat to 375°. Grease a teaspoon by dipping into hot fat. Spoon up some of the batter, and drop into pan. Repeat, dipping the spoon each time. Turn when cakes rise to top, and continue frying until brown on both sides. Spoon out with slotted spoon, and drain on paper towels. Cooking time: 2-3 minutes. Yield: About 24 small cakes.

Southern Berry Pies

1½ cups all-purpose flour
½ teaspoon salt
½ cup shortening
¼ cup thick raspberry preserves
Confectioner's sugar
Oil for pan ½" deep

Combine flour and salt, cut in shortening, and gradually add about 3 tablespoons cold water to hold mixture together. Gather dough into ball, then roll out ⅛-inch thick. Cut pastry dough into 3-inch circles. In the center of each place a teaspoon of raspberry preserves. Fold. Seal edges by pressing down with a fork. Add oil to pan.

Heat pan to 380°. As soon as light goes off, add pies, a single layer at a time and fry until golden. Remove and drain on absorbent paper. While still warm, shake in paper bag containing confectioner's sugar. Cooking time: 3-5 minutes. Yield: 12 small pies.

Variation—Make 3-inch squares of the dough as above. Place a teaspoon of orange marmalade, thick applesauce, or cooked puréed prunes in each square. Fold, and seal edges with a fork. Fry as in the recipe above.

Christmas Cookies

Skillet-fried cookies are light and delicious.

> 3 egg yolks
> 3 tablespoons sugar
> Dash of cinnamon
> 3 tablespoons heavy cream
> 1 teaspoon brandy (optional)
> 1¼ cups sifted all-purpose flour
> Oil for pan ¾" deep
> Confectioner's sugar

Beat egg yolks until thick and lemon-colored. Add sugar, cinnamon and cream, and continue beating until thickened. Add brandy. Stir in flour gradually to make a smooth dough. Roll out very thin. Cut into strips 1½-inches wide. Cut strips diagonally every 3 inches. Make 1-inch slit in center and slip one end of dough through the slit to form a bow. Put shortening in pan.

Heat pan to 350°. Using a slotted spoon, place bows in the hot fat and fry until delicately brown. Remove, and drain on paper towels. Sprinkle with confectioner's sugar while still hot. Cooking time: 1½-2 minutes. Yield: About 36 cookies.

Skillet Peach Brown Betty

¼ cup butter or margarine
8 slices day-old bread, cubed
½ cup brown sugar
1⅓ cups applesauce
½ teaspoon cinnamon
Dash of salt
½ cup broken walnuts or pecans

Heat pan to 300°. Melt butter or margarine. Brown bread on all sides, turning as necessary and stirring frequently. Combine sugar, applesauce, cinnamon, salt and nuts. Pour into pan, and heat for 10 minutes. Serve warm with hard sauce or cream. Cooking time: About 15 minutes. Yield: 4 servings.

Hard Sauce. Cream together 3 tablespoons butter or margarine, ½ cup confectioner's sugar and ¼ teaspoon vanilla.

Easy Apple Fritters

1 cup all-purpose flour
1½ teaspoons baking powder
¼ teaspoon salt
⅓ cup milk
1 egg, slightly beaten
2 or 3 tart apples
Oil for pan ¾" deep

Combine flour, baking powder and salt, then stir in milk and egg. Pare, core, and dice apples. Combine with batter. Put oil into pan.

Heat pan to 370°. Drop apple batter by tablespoonsful into hot fat. Cook until brown, turning as necessary. Remove with slotted spoon. Drain on absorbent paper. Serve with maple sirup, or sprinkle with cinnamon. Cool oil; store for later use. Cooking time: 2-4 minutes. Yield: 4-6 servings.

Fruit Flambé

This is the easiest possible dessert but it is fun to watch and unusual enough to honor your culinary ability. Heat in skillet with a few tablespoons brandy any good frozen fruit melange, adding canned fruits to extend the quantity. Warm a few tablespoons of rum in a butter melter or small saucepan. Set it ablaze at the table and pour it into the skillet, (turn the temperature off just before you do this). Serve fruit and sauce with sour cream. Good over plain cake too.

Blazing Cherries Jubilee

How to add drama to an ordinary dinner.

1 No. 2 can black sweet cherries, pitted
1 tablespoon cornstarch
2 tablespoons cold water
½ cup Kirsch liqueur

Drain sirup from cherries into pan. Heat to 380°. Let sirup boil for a few minutes.

Reduce heat to 200°. Combine cornstarch diluted in cold water, stir into sirup, add cherries and simmer until cherries are thoroughly heated. Turn off heat, disconnect pan. Pour in Kirsch, set ablaze, and spoon onto ice cream or pudding while still blazing. Cooking time: 10 minutes. Yield: 4 servings.

Stewed Oranges

Peel 6 navel oranges. Save the peel. Remove membrane from the oranges and section them. Scrape off white pulp from peel, then cut enough peel to make 2 tablespoons of fine slivers. Add 1 cup sugar and ½ cup water. Cook at medium heat for 8 minutes until sirupy. Pour hot sirup over uncooked orange sections. Refrigerate until ready to use. Good over ice cream.

Fruit Fritters

This is good also for apple rings, pear slices, banana and peach chunks.

> 1 cup pitted prunes
> 1 cup dried apricots
> ½ cup sugar
> 1 cup all-purpose flour
> 1 teaspoon baking powder
> ½ teaspoon salt
> 2 teaspoons melted butter or oil
> 1 egg, slightly beaten
> 6 tablespoons water
> Confectioner's sugar
> Oil for pan ¾" deep

Cook prunes and apricots until tender in water that just barely covers them. Allow about 25 minutes. In last 5 minutes, add all but 2 tablespoons sugar. Now make a batter: Combine remainder of sugar, flour, baking powder, salt with butter, egg, and water (just enough to make a thick batter). Mix well. Dip fruit in batter, let excess drain. Add oil to pan.

Heat pan to 380°. Drop fritters into hot fat and fry until brown on all sides. Remove with slotted spoon, and drain immediately on absorbent paper to keep them crisp. Sprinkle with confectioner's sugar. Serve with a tart lemon sauce. Cooking time: 12-18 minutes. Yield: About 25 fritters.

Poaching Fruit

Put canned fruit into strainer held over skillet. When sirup goes through, set strainer and fruit aside and cook sirup for 10 minutes at 250°. Taste for sweetness, adding sugar as necessary. Turn in fruit and let cook for 3 minutes. Good with a cold buffet. Poach the fruit at the table.

Kumquat Garnish for Pineapple

Pierce a hole in the stem side of a quart of kumquats. Cover with cold water in the skillet, bring to quick boil, then lower heat to simmering temperature and cook about 20 minutes. Drain. Add 1 cup water and 1 cup sugar to skillet, cook kumquats at 275°, turning them in sirup so that they become well coated and glazed. Chill, then stick them into the centers of pineapple squares in an attractive pattern. (First cut off the leafy pineapple top. Cut out pineapple with melon ball scoop. Return balls to pineapple shell, add a few tablespoons of sherry and some sugar if needed, and return leafy top. Pineapple stuck with kumquats, resting on a few green leaves, makes an attractive edible centerpiece for a buffet table.)

Large Pineapple Upside Down Cake

The Reynolds Aluminum Home Economics staff suggested the use of foil in upside-down cake. It works beautifully, and the cake is easier to remove than if baked right in the pan.

    5 tablespoons butter
    ¾ cup brown sugar
    12-14 canned pineapple slices
    12-14 pecan halves
    ⅓ cup shortening
    1 cup granulated sugar
    2 eggs, beaten
    2 cups flour
    2 teaspoons baking powder
    ¼ teaspoon salt
    ½ cup milk mixed with
    ¼ cup pineapple sirup and
    1 teaspoon vanilla flavoring

Line 12" frypan with 18" heavy duty aluminum foil extending extra foil over the outside of the pan. Melt butter in pan set at 250°. As soon as butter is melted stir in brown sugar. Mix well with a rubber spatula. (Handle carefully so as not to tear the foil). Arrange pineapple slices over butter-sugar spread. Put a pecan in each pineapple center. (Extra pecan halves may be arranged between slices.) Turn temperature off.

Cream shortening, add sugar gradually, then add eggs and beat well. Stir flour, baking powder and salt together. Add them alternately with milk-sirup mixture to egg mixture. Beat well after each addition. Spread batter evenly over the mixture in the frypan.

Turn heat to 275°. Cover pan, open vent and bake for ½ hour (the cake will spring back when lightly touched). Place a large plate over pan, and invert to remove. Peel off aluminum foil, pressing back any pineapple which may be stuck to foil. This is an attractive, easy to do cake. Serves 12-14.

Hot Coffee-Chocolate

Put 2 squares unsweetened chocolate and 1 cup water in a skillet set at 250°. Stir until chocolate melts and mixture is smooth, then add 3 tablespoons sugar, a dash of cinnamon and 3 cups milk. Add 3 cups strong coffee and heat until steaming but do not let it boil. Ladle into coffee mugs and serve either plain or with whipped cream. Serves 8. A good winter drink. Serve with a simple cake as a 4 o'clock refreshment.

Café Brûlot

This is a theatrical after-dinner beverage to be made at the table with most of the lights turned off. I especially like to do it outdoors and serve it at garden parties when the main course has been cleared away and it is already dark. There is usually just enough breeze to make this very hot coffee very welcome. Incidentally, take note that you do not need a special café brûlot bowl—your skillet does the job quite well.

1½ cups brandy
1 thin slice lemon peel cut in a continuous spiral (do not include any of the white part)
1 thin slice orange peel cut in a continuous spiral (do not include any of the white part)
8 lumps sugar
8 whole cloves
3 sticks cinnamon
8 cups strong black coffee (strong instant coffee works well too)

Put everything except the coffee in the skillet heated to 250°. Turn off heat. Set the brandy on fire. Extinguish the blaze by pouring in the coffee, mix thoroughly and serve very hot. If necessary reheat by setting skillet at simmering temperature. Do not let boil. Ladle (use a silver one if you have it) into demitasses or ordinary coffee cups. Serves 8 to 10. If you do not pour all the coffee immediately, it can be kept hot in a skillet set at 180°. Makes a dramatic coffee to serve at a Christmas party.

INDEX

A

à la meuniere, 59
Almonds, toasted, 30
Apple fritters, 185
  pancakes, 168
  sauce, 181
Apples with fruit filling, 181
  pommes sauté, 181
Asparagus, 135
  ham and egg casserole, 136

B

Bacon, pan-broiled, 103
  tomato and peanut butter
    buns, 177
Banana pancakes, 168
Barbecue sauce, 44
Barbecued beefburgers, 174
  chicken in foil, 111
Beans
  chili con carne, 139
Beef
  filet Stroganov, 83
  hamburger mixed grill, 89
  hash, 87
  Italian meat balls, 91
  meat loaf casserole, 89
    ring, 88
  pimentos stuffed with, 92
  pot roast with gingersnap
    gravy, 87
  roast, sandwich, 176
  shepherd's pies, 90
  steak au poivre, 81
    Chinese pepper, 82
    rolled steak wheels, 82
  stew and vegetables, 88
    olive and potato ragout, 86
  suki-yaki, 84
  Swedish meat balls, 90
  tongue, sweet and sour, 94
Beets, 135
Beurre noir, 45
Beverages, 189-190
  café brulot, 190
  coffee-chocolate, 189
Bigarde sauce, 45
Bitochki, 28
Blintzes, 177
Blueberry pancakes, 168

Bouillabaisse, 41
Brains, sautéed, 95
Braising, 15
Bread
  buttered, 173
  to freshen rolls, 172
  to heat, 173
Broccoli, 137
Brown sauce, 44
Brussels sprouts, 135, 137
Butterfly shrimp, 29

C

Cabbage, 135
  and apple casserole, 138
Café brûlot, 190
Cake
  pineapple upside down, 188
  tea, 183
Canapé bases, 31
Cantonese spareribs, 107
Carolina chicken pilau, 116
Carrots, 145
Cauliflower, 135, 138
Celery, 140
  bisque, 38
Chafing dish cookery, 17
Champagne raisin sauce, 50
Cheese
  and tomato sandwich, 176
  blintzes, 177
  grilled American, 178
  hors d'oeuvres, 24
  pancakes, 169
  ring tum tiddy, 163
  sauce, 42
  Welsh rarebit, 164
Cherries jubilee, 186
Cherry sauce, 46
Chicken, 109-132
  à la king, 120
  and gravy sandwiches, 174
  and ham skewers, 131
  and spaghetti casserole, 125
  barbecued, 111
  batter-fried, 113
  braised with sherry wine, 117
  breast of, 124
  cacciatore, 119
  Carolina chicken pilau, 116

Chicken, *continued*
  Chinese diced and almonds, 123
  chow mein, 127
  coq au vin, 129
  croquettes, 128
  curry in avocado, 130
  dinner in a skillet, 111
  divan, 124
  drumsticks, stuffed, 125
  egg drop soup, 37
  fricassee for four, 119
  giblets, 46, 127
  hash, 112
  Hungarian, with sour cream, 116
  in a ring, 112
  in fruit, 122
  livers with fresh apple rings, 93
  paella, 115
  pies, 126
  pollo con arroz, 114
  soup, 36
  southern fried, 112
  stew with dumplings, 118
  sukiyaki, 120
Chiles rellenos, 145
Chinese diced chicken and
    almonds, 123
  egg rolls, 27
Chocolate fudge sauce, 47
  sauce, 47
Chow mein, 127
Christmas cookies, 184
Clam chowder, 39
  fritters, 66
  newburg, 64
Cleaning the skillet, 13
Cocktail frankfurters and
    pineapple, 29
  turnovers, 25
Codfish cakes, 56
Coffee-chocolate, 189
Coffee sauce, 48
Cookies, Christmas, 184
Coq au vin Chateaubriand, 129
Corn on the cob, 139
  fritters, 140
Court bouillon, 59
Crab cakes Maryland, 65
  stew, 65
Crab meat au sherry, 66

Crabs, soft-shell, 65
Cream sauce, 43
Creamed turkey on toast, 176
Croque monsieur, 175
Croquettes,
  chicken, 128
  lobster, 28
Cucumber sauce, 43
Cucumbers, 141
Curry (chicken) in avocado, 130
  sauce, 43

D

Deep frying procedure, 14
Desserts, 179-188
  apple fritters, 185
    pommes sauté, 181
    sauce, 181
    with fruit filling, 181
  brandied peaches, 182
  cherries jubilee, 186
  fruit flambé, 186
    fritters, 187
    sauce, 182
  oranges, stewed, 187
  peach brown betty, 185
    brandied, 182
  pears in wine, 182
  pies, Southern berry, 183
  pineapple upside down cake, 188
  tea cakes, 183
Dough strips, 32
Duck in vermouth, 131
  mandarin, 132
Dumplings,
  chicken stew with, 118
  in lamb stew, 102

E

Egg and Cheese Dishes, 157-164
Eggplant
  French fried, 142
  luncheon for four, 141
Egg rolls, 27
Eggs
  and zucchini sauté, 161
  baked, 160
  creamed, 160
  foo yoong, 162
  fried, 159

in a nest, 161
omelet roll, ham filled, 163
poached, 159
scrambled, 160
shirred, 160
sunnyside, 159
Western sandwich, 175

F

Fish and Shellfish, 53-78
à la meuniere, 59
and chips, 57
clam fritters, 66
newburg, 64
codfish cakes, 56
court bouillon for, 69
crab cakes, 65
au sherry, 66
soft shell, 65
stew, 65
deep frying, 55
dinner, 63
flounder fillets, 60
au vin, 58
haddock and mushrooms en
brochette, 63
halibut and oyster ragout, 62
loaf, 56
lobster
Cantonese, 75
Margarita, 76
newburg, 74
and shrimp patties, 77
oysters in blankets, 68
fry, 67
terrapin, 68
salmon scalloped, 78
scallops sautéed, 69
shallow frying, 55
shrimps
Fra diavolo, 70
French fried, 72
jambalaya, 74
marinara, 71
steamed, 71
with green peas and rice, 72
steaks with white grapes, 61
sticks, 57
tuna casserole, 61
Florentine sauce, 51

Flounder au vin, 58
Frankfurters and bean
casserole, 105
and cabbage, 105
and pineapple, 29
French toast, 173
sandwiches, 174
Fricassee for four, chicken, 119
Fritters
apple, 185
fruit, 187
Fritto misto, 30
Fruit, *see also by name*
chicken in, 122
flambé, 186
fritters, 187
poaching, 187
sauce, 50, 182

G

Giblets, 127
gravy, 46
stock, 46
Grilling, 16

H

Haddock and mushroom en
brochette, 63
Halibut and oyster ragout, 62
Ham
and chicken skewers, 131
and potato skillet, 103
egg, and banana grill, 163
pineapple-hamburger, 103
Hamburger
meat balls in onion sauce, 23
mixed grill, 89
Hash, 87, 112
Hollandaise sauce, mock, 43
Hors d'oeuvres, 21-32
almonds, toasted, 30
bitochki, 27
buffet meat balls in onion
sauce, 23
butterfly shrimp, 29
canapé bases, 31
cheese, 24
Chinese egg rolls, 27
cocktail frankfurters and
pineapple, 25

Hors d'oeuvres, *continued*
  dough strips, 32
  fritto misto, 30
  knishes, liver, 30
  lobster croquettes, 28
  olive and bacon rolls, 24
  oysters in bacon blankets, 27
  pop corn, 31
  teriyakis, 31
  Turkish pepper with yogurt
    dressing, 23
Hungarian chicken with sour
  cream, 116

I
Italian meat balls, 91

K
Kasha, 143
Knishes, liver, 26
Kumquat garnish, 188

L
Lamb, 99-102
  chops in Burgundy, 99
    pan-broiled, 100
    roquefort, 100
  cutlets, breaded, 100
  rolls, Turkish, 101
  stew with dumplings, 102
    Patlijian, 101
Lasagne, 154
Lemon sauce, 48
Liver and mushroom skewers, 93
  knishes, 26
  sautéed in wine, 94
Lobster
  and shrimp patties, 77
  Cantonese, 75
  croquettes, 28
  Margarita, 76
  newburg, 74
  sauce, 60

M
Maple sundae sauce, 49
Matzo dumplings, 37
Meat balls
  in onion sauce, 23
  Italian, 91
Meat loaf casserole, 89
  ring, 88

Melba sauce, 49
Minestrone, 35
Mushroom sauce, 45

O
Olive and bacon rolls, 24
Onion soup, French, 38
Onions
  batter-fried, 144
  crisp fried, 144
  glazed, 144
Oranges, stewed, 187
Orange sauce, 48
Oyster fry, 67
  in blanket, 27
  terrapin, 68

P
Paella, 115
Pan broiling, 16
Pancakes, 165-171
  apple, 168
  banana, 168
  basic, 168
  blueberry, 168
  buckwheat, 169
  buttermilk, 169
  cheese, 169
  crêpes suzette, 170
  filled, 171
  Hawaiian, 169
  potato, 171
  strawberry, 169
  Tahiti, 169
  tuna fish and cottage cheese, 172
Peach brown betty, 185
Peaches, brandied, 182
Pears in wine, 182
Peas à la bonne femme, 144
Peppers, chiles rellenos, 145
Pies
  chicken, deep-fried, 126
  Southern berry, 183
Pimentos, beef stuffed, 92
Pineapple rice, 130
  upside down cake, 188
Poaching, 16
  fruit, 187
Pop corn, 31
Pollo con arroz, 114

Pork, 106-108
  bacon, 103
  chop casserole, 106
    sweet cherries and, 106
  spareribs, barbecued, 108
    Cantonese, 107
  sausage, 104, 107
Pot roast with gingersnap gravy, 87
Pot roasting, 15
Potato pancakes, 171
Potatoes, 146-149
  croquettes, 149
  curls, 147
  French-fried, 146
    in two parts, 147
    frozen, 148
  German fried, 148
  hashed brown, 147
  marbles, 146
  salad, hot, 149
  shoestring, 146
  souffléed, 148

R

Ratatouille, 156
Rice, 150-152
  and raisin patties, 151
  fluffy, 150
  fritters, 150
  mold, 151
  pineapple, 130
  shrimp fried, 152
Ring tum tiddy, 163
Roast beef sandwich, 176
Roux, 45

S

Salmon, scalloped, 78
Saltimbocca, 97
Sandwich steaks, 174
Sandwiches, 174-178
  American cheese, grilled, 178
  bacon, tomato and peanut
    butter, 177
  beefburgers, barbecued, 174
  cheese and tomato, 176
  chicken and gravy, 174
  club specials, 175
  croque monsieur, 175
  roast beef, 176

  steak, 174
  turkey, creamed, 176
  western, 175
Sauces, 42-51
  barbecue, 44
  basic brown, 44
  beurre noir, 45
  bigarde, 45
  champagne raisin, 50
  cheese, 42
  chocolate, 47
    fudge, 47
  coffee, 48
  cream, 43
  cucumber, 43
  curry, 43
  florentine, 51
  fruit, 50
  hard, 185
  lemon, 48
  maple sundae, 49
  maraschino cherry, 46
  melba, 49
  mock hollandaise, 43
  mushroom, 45
  orange, 48
  roux for, 45
  sherry, 49
  spaghetti, 51
  tartar, hot, 43
  velouté, 52
  white, 42
Sausages, 104
  and baked bean casserole, 107
Sautéing, 15
Scallops sautéed, 69
Scampi marinara, 71
Schnitzel à la Holstein, 97
Shallow frying, 15
Shepherd's pies, 90
Sherry sauce, 49
Shrimp
  butterfly, 29
  Fra Diavolo in rice ring, 70
  French fried, 72
  fried rice, 152
  gumbo, 40
  jambalaya, 74
  steamed, 71
  with green peas and rice, 72

Simmering, 17
Soups, 35-41
  bouillabaisse, 41
  celery bisque, 38
  chicken, 36
    egg drop, 37
  clam chowder, 39
  minestrone, 35
  onion soup, 38
  shrimp gumbo, 40
Southern berry pies, 183
Southern-Fried Chicken, 112
Spaghetti sauce, 51
Spinach, 135
  and noodle casserole, 153
  patties, 152
Squash, 145
Steak
  au poivre, 81
  Chinese pepper, 82
  rolled steak wheels, 82
Stewing, 17
Suki-yaki, 84, 120
Swedish meat balls, 90
Sweetbreads and mushrooms, 95
Sweet potatoes
  and pineapple puffs, 153
  fried, 153

T

Tartar sauce, hot, 43
  quick, 69
Tea cakes, 183
Temperatures, 19
Tempura, 73
Teriyakis, 31
Tomatoes
  provençale, 154
  sautéed zucchini with, 155
Tongue, sweet and sour, 94
Tuna casserole, 61
  and cottage cheese
    pancakes, 172
Turkish pepper with Yogurt
  dressing, 23
Turkey creamed on toast, 176
Turnovers, cocktail, 25

U

Using the skillet, 12

V

Veal, 96-99
  breaded, 96
  casserole, 99
  chops with herbs, 98
  Milanese, 97
  mozzarella, 96
  parmigiana, 96
  saltimbocca, 97
  scallopini, 96
  schnitzel à la Holstein, 96
  stew, 98
  wiener schnitzel, 96
Vegetables, 133-155
  asparagus, 135, 136
  beans (chili con carne), 139
  broccoli, 137
  Brussels sprouts, 135, 137
  cabbage, 135, 138
  cauliflower, 135, 138
  celery, 140
  corn, 139, 140
  cucumbers, 141
  eggplant, 141, 142
  kasha, 143
  lasagne, 154
  onions, 144
  peas, 144
  peppers, 145
  potatoes, 146-149
  ratatouille, 156
  rice, 150-152
  spinach, 135, 152, 153
  sweet potatoes, 153
  tomatoes, 154
  zucchini, 155
Velouté sauce, 52

W

Warming foods, 18
Welsh rarebit, 164
Western sandwich, 175
White sauce, 42
Wiener schnitzel, 97

Z

Zucchini, 155
  and egg sauté, 161